THE KATHMANDU VALLEY

Author John Sanday spent ten years in Kathmandu restoring historic buildings for UNESCO. He is currently working for the Getty Foundation in California, and will soon be working on a project restoring Tibetan Buddhist monuments in western Sichuan, People's Republic of China.

THE KATHMANDU VALLEY

John Sanday

PASSPORT BOOKS
a division of *NTC Publishing Group*
Lincolnwood, Illinois USA

Published by Passport Books in conjunction with
The Guidebook Company Ltd.

This edition first published in 1995 by Passport Books, a division of NTC Publishing Group,
4255 W. Touhy Avenue, Lincolnwood (Chicago), Illinois 60646-1975 USA.
Originally published by The Guidebook Company Ltd.

ISBN: 0-8442-9953-7
Library of Congress Catalog Number: 93-83312

Series Editors: Bikram Grewel, May Holdsworth, Ralph Kiggell
and Toby Sinclair
Contributing Editor: Tom Le Bas
Picture Editor: Carolyn Watts
Map Artwork: Bai Yiliang
Illustrations: Patrick Troch
Design: Angela Hyder and Janice Lee

ISBN: 962-217-196-6

Photography: Helka Ahokas 12–13, 16–17, 32–3, 52–3, 92–3, 147; Dean Barrett, Images (57); Earl Kowall (44, 61 both, 74–5 all three); Pat Lam (40 both, 143); John Sanday (78, 105, 126, 131, 168, 172 both, 186); Bill Wassman (5, 9, 20, 37, 41, 70, 85, 96–7, 109, 122–3, 134, 138–9, 151, 158–9, 179, 183, 191); Steve Van Beek (28, 115)

Production House: Twin Age Ltd, Hong Kong
Printed in Hong Kong by Sing Cheong Printing Co Ltd

Contents

One of the four Ashoka stupas, *Patan*

Maps

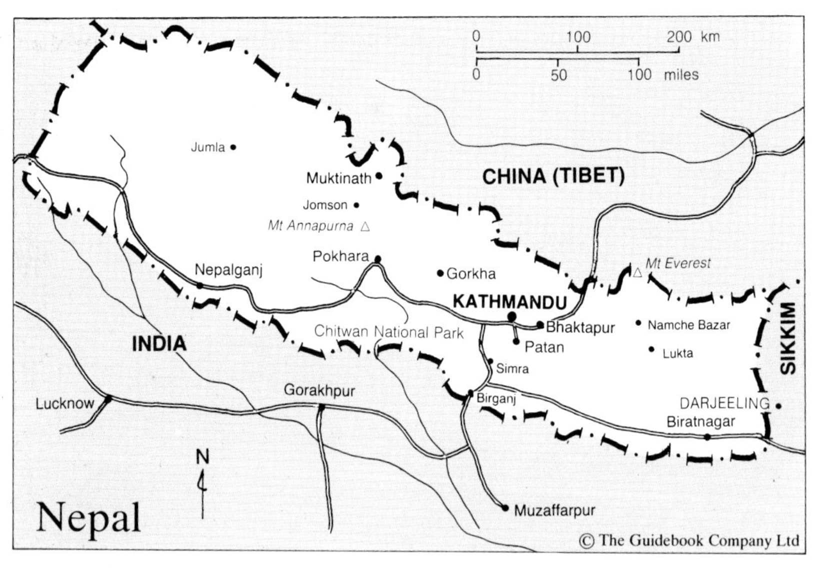

Preface

This guidebook is intended to be different from the standard guide you will find on Nepal as it stems from my 17 years of experience in the unique and much treasured environment of the Kathmandu Valley. It is a compilation of the experiences I have gained from living and working among the craftsmen of the Valley as an architect-restorer. During my first seven years there, I worked as a UNESCO adviser to the Nepali Government, where I established the first major building conservation project in the old royal palace known as the Hanuman Dhoka in the centre of Kathmandu. I built up a team of over 200 local craftsmen and together we studied traditional Nepali methods of construction. With the knowledge we gained, we developed ways of conserving and repairing the massive timber beams which were the frameworks of these buildings and which had been distorted by a series of earthquakes; and learnt how to piece in and repair the damaged woodcarvings.

Earthquakes have occurred throughout history on a major scale more or less every 40 years. In 1934, there was a disastrous quake which caused untold damage in the Kathmandu Valley following a previous sizeable tremor in the early 1890s. In 1988 there was a serious earthquake in the lowlands of Nepal causing damage and loss of life in districts beyond the Valley. Luckily no historic structures were seriously damaged in this quake.

The conservation project was a shared learning experience: I helped the craftsmen to develop an awareness of their unique architectural heritage, while they introduced me to and shared their crafts, customs and religion. We became a close-knit team—an extended family, as the many other projects we later worked on together were based on our experiences at Hanuman Dhoka.

A few years ago in Kathmandu, I and some fellow architects formed a consultancy firm which pooled the experience we had gained from living and working with the Nepali craftsmen. The practice is now designing and constructing buildings with a traditional quality.

This is why the guide has a strong architectural flavour and why it shares with you some of my experiences gained from the Hanuman Dhoka project. It is also based on the 'tours' I gave my friends through the Kathmandu Valley, during which I endeavoured to create the appropriate ambience for them while exploring the many villages in the surrounding countryside. These tours became a popular introduction to Nepal's cultural heritage for expatriates. Their theme was 'Use Your Eyes!' as I found people gained great enjoyment from discovering and sharing their experiences. I hope this book will help you, as you wander through this stunning and unique cultural microcosm, to raise your eyes and experience above and beyond the normal guided tour.

Introduction

On one of the many journeys I made beyond the Kathmandu Valley into the hills, I vividly remember encountering a wizened old Sherpa lady striding along the trail towards me with a great sense of purpose but apparently miles from anywhere. We greeted one another and, following normal custom in the hills, engaged in a lengthy exchange of questions. I asked her where she was going and she replied 'Nepal'. I asked her again, 'Where are you going?' Again she replied, 'Nepal', adding that it would take her three days to reach her destination. It was only then that I realized she was, in fact, referring to the Kathmandu Valley, which to her and to many people of her generation *is* the Kingdom of Nepal.

For centuries, traders, explorers and travellers have struggled on foot and horseback through the lowland Terai and up the old Rajpath which, through India, links Nepal with the outside world. Or they have come over one of the numerous high passes between Nepal and Tibet to reach the Kathmandu Valley, then as now the fulcrum on which all activity in Nepal turns, whether economic, political, social or cultural, and from where all influences, past and prevailing, have come.

Because of its long years of inaccessibility and difficulties of communication and travel within the country even today, much of Nepal has remained unspoilt and it is this, and the very isolation of most parts of the country, that enhances its magical appeal and draws the traveller to this unique Himalayan stronghold.

As your time in Nepal will probably be limited, many of you will have to accept, as the old Sherpa lady did, that the Kathmandu Valley *is* Nepal. However, I hope that, with this book as your travel companion, you will be able to witness and feel more deeply the true atmosphere and character of this unusual kingdom.

The guide opens with a short account of the history, ecology and physical characteristics of the Valley and a brief description of its architecture. Then follows a series of tours, with details of the buildings, crafts and traditions you will encounter on each of them.

Sadly, these townscapes you have travelled thousands of miles to see are slowly disintegrating as a result of the effects of time and the harsh weather conditions. Efforts to save them are being made. There is now an established cadre of craftsmen who, with their local traditional knowledge enhanced by the various training programmes undertaken by UNESCO and other funding agencies, can effectively handle restoration and conservation. Finance, however, is still being sought to undertake the daunting task of conserving the thousands of buildings that constitute the kaleidoscopic fabric of the Kathmandu Valley.

Facts for the Traveller

Visas

As of July 1994 Nepal's visa procedures are as follows: **visas available at Kathmandu International airport** (i) 48 hour transit visa, US$5, must present an airline ticket confirming departure within 24 hours of arrival, (ii) single entry tourist visa for 15 days, US$15, (iii) single entry tourist visa for 30 days, US$25, (iv) double entry tourist visa for 30 days, valid for 2 months from issue date, US$40, (v) multiple entry tourist visa for 60 days, valid for 2 months from issue date, US$60. Visas are also available from **Nepali embassies and consulates**; these are the same as those available at the airport, except that double and multiple entry visas are valid for 6 months instead of 2, from issue date. Visas can be extended up to 150 days at a rate of US$1 per day.

Customs

You are permitted to import the standard quantities of tobacco and alcohol. However, there are restrictions on importing electronic goods and you may find that certain items such as video cameras and tape recorders may be noted in your passport to ensure you take them home with you. Special permits are required for 16mm cameras.

Controls are strict at Tribhuvan Airport and baggage is usually thoroughly checked on entry.

You must also clear customs on departure and you should be aware of the following regulations:

- Souvenirs can be exported freely but any item that is over 100 years old must have an export certificate from the Department of Archaeology.
- Wild animals or skins cannot be exported without a licence and CITES certificate.
- There are also currency controls and it is forbidden to import or export Nepalese rupees. Keep the currency card sometimes issued by customs on arrival ready for inspection
- Make sure you have a valid visa as you can be penalized if it is out of date.

Climate

Set at an elevation of 1,350 metres (4,500 feet), the Kathmandu Valley enjoys a pleasant climate with distinct seasons. Winter, from October to March, sees cool nights (cold in January when temperatures can reach freezing) and glorious sunny, warm days when the air is fresh and clear. At this time there is often an early morning mist which normally clears by around 10 am to leave the rest of the day sunny.

Spring, from April to late June, can be hot and close with dramatic thunderstorms at night. The Kathmandu Valley is in full bloom but the landscape and mountain views are often hazy due to the heat. The pre-monsoon rains periodically clear the air. Temperatures will vary between 10°C (50°F) and 28°C (82°F), but can rise to over 30°C (86°F) during late May and early June.

The summer, or monsoon, spans the rainy season from mid-June to the end of September. The rains are normally heavy at the start of the monsoon and gradually decrease. The sun usually makes a brief appearance each day and the cloud formations and light effects are spectacular. Humidity is high but the temperature drops during the rainstorms.

Clothing

Unless you are on official business, dress in Kathmandu is very informal. For daytime wear, light clothing is recommended. Cottons are preferable as synthetic fibres can cause irritation to the skin. In the evening you will require a heavy woollen sweater (lovely ones can be bought cheaply in Kathmandu) or anorak. Excessive exposure of the legs by both sexes is somewhat frowned upon, so jeans or long skirts are in order and sensible comfortable shoes essential. Umbrellas which are very cheap locally are best against the rains. If you are travelling beyond the Valley you will need alpine gear (available for rent in many shops in Kathmandu) for trekking in the mountains plus a good sun hat. For the Terai it can be cold at night during the winter months and it is advisable to take a sweater.

Health

No vaccinations or inoculations are currently required for entry into Nepal. However, it is recommended that you are immunized against hepatitis, typhoid, cholera and tetanus. It is best to discuss your needs with your doctor well in advance of your trip. Protection against malaria in the Kathmandu Valley is not necessary, though it is advisable if you are travelling to the Terai. However, bring a mosquito repellent for the warmer months as the non-malaria breed is to be found in abundance. There are plenty of drug stores selling mostly Indian products with which you can supplement your own medical kit. Bring your own high-factor sun barriers.

Never drink unboiled or unfiltered water, and forgo ice cubes. Avoid eating raw vegetables and unpeeled fruit—most diseases are waterborne and good-quality water is not one of the Valley's strong points. Do not walk around barefoot, and wash your hands before eating. If you follow these simple rules you may avoid the typical 'Kathmandu Tummy'. However, an upset tummy may just be a normal sign that your body is adjusting, and should only last a few days. There are several doctors well versed in both

Western and Eastern medicine who are skilled in treating such disorders should you be struck down with intestinal or other health problems.

Money

Nepali currency is the rupee, which has a different value from the Indian rupee. The currency comes in 1,000, 500, 100, 50, 10, 5, 2 and 1 rupee notes. 100 paisa make up a rupee and there are 1 rupee coins, and 50, 25, 10 and 5 paisa coins. Money can be exchanged at the airport on arrival, in most banks, and at some hotels. The official rate of exchange was about Rs48 to the US Dollar in late 1994. Banks are open Sunday to Thursday from 10 am to 3 pm and on Fridays from 10 am to noon. Try to avoid ending up with torn notes in your change, as locals are often unwilling to accept them.

You may bring in any amount of currency but you must declare amounts over US$2,000 in cash on arrival. Most international credit cards are accepted.

Tipping is becoming common practice and a few rupees work wonders. However, do not overtip and only give if a service has been rendered. It is not necessary to tip taxi drivers other than rounding up the paisa to a rupee.

Local Transport

There are several means of local transport ranging from taxis to bicycles, public buses to minibuses, or the local means of travel—by foot!

Taxis The taxi cab is easily recognizable as it has a yellow roof and black number plates. Taxis have meters but rarely seem to use them; if you negotiate, cut the offered price by 50 percent and work from there. Generally, costs are reasonable and it seldom needs more than a few dollars to reach any destination in Kathmandu or Patan. Daily charges for a taxi will be in the region of Rs1000 per day. You can hire private cars from travel agents for between US$30 and US$75 per day. Petrol is also expensive.

Scooters The three-wheeled scooter or *tempo* is either public (running a standard route) or private (like a small, extremely uncomfortable but cheap taxi).

Rickshaws The next best thing to walking is a ride through the town on a rickshaw—the slow-moving, bell-ringing, brightly-painted form of local transport. The rates should be cheaper than a taxi but for a tourist seldom are! Always settle the fare before you mount the vehicle and make sure both you and the rickshaw-wallah know where you are going.

Bicycles Cycling is the best way of seeing the Kathmandu Valley. Bicycles can be hired all over town for about Rs50 per day. Check your mount before you set off and ensure that the brakes and bell work and that the tyres are in good order.

On Foot Be prepared for a lot of walking, both through the towns and out in the fields, as most of the interesting sites are off the beaten track. Walking is certainly the best way to assimilate the atmosphere of the Kathmandu Valley. You will be quite safe to wander off into the fields where the local farmers will welcome you and help you to discover the charm of the people and countryside.

Communication

Nepal has its own earth satellite station so international telephone and telex communication is remarkably good. Mail, cables and local phone calls, on the other hand, can produce a great deal of frustration.

Mail There is an international post office (open 10 am–5 pm except Saturdays and holidays) in Sundhara, at the southwestern end of the Tundhikel, with a poste restante service (open 10 am–4 pm). An American Express mail service is located close to Durbar Marg. Bank transactions are best done by telegraphic transfers to a foreign bank with a branch in Kathmandu. Nepali banks take a long time to issue your money.

Telecommunications Most hotels are connected to the international direct-dialling network, so phoning around the world is simple. There are several private phone and fax bureaux throughout the valley, providing a good service at reasonable cost. One can also use the public telephone system at the international telecommunications building opposite the national stadium in Tripureswar. Dial 180 for calls within Nepal, 187 for calls to India, 197 for enquiries and 186 for international calls.

Newspapers and books The most popular English-language daily newspapers printed in Kathmandu are the *Rising Nepal* and the *Kathmandu Post*. International and national news coverage is adequate. Indian newspapers are also available, and the *International Herald Tribune* and certain international magazines can be found in some bookstalls. There are plenty of good bookshops in Kathmandu, selling new and secondhand books.

Time

Time Zones Nepal has its own special time zone which is 15 minutes ahead of India and five hours 45 minutes ahead of Greenwich Mean Time.

The Calendar Although there are five different calendars in use in Nepal, the official one, known as the Vikram Sambat, is used most frequently. The first year of this calendar corresponds to 57 BC of the Western Gregorian calendar, thus 1995 and 1996 in the West are 2052 and 2053 in Nepal. There are also 12 months in the Vikram calendar; the first month begins in mid-April with the Nepali New Year. The months are Baisakh (April/May), Jesth (May/June), Asadh (June/July), Srawan (July/August)

Ashwin (September/October), Kartik (October/November), Marga (November/December, Poush (December/January), Magha (January/February), Falgun (February/March), and Chaitra (March/April). (For National Festivals, see page 175.)

Working Hours The business week begins on Sunday, as Saturday is the rest day. Offices work from 10 am to 5 pm in summer and to 4 pm in winter. Friday is a half day and government offices close at 1 pm. Most shops are open from 10 am until 8 pm or later. Bank hours are 10 am to 2:30 pm Sunday to Thursday, 10 am to 12:30 pm on Friday.

Photography

Bring all the film you think you will need as it is only available in Kathmandu and is fairly expensive. Many places can develop film reliably and quickly by machine. You can buy camera equipment, but again at a price!

Physical Environment

The Kathmandu Valley, drained by the holy Bagmati, is almost as broad as it is wide, and covers an area of 570 square kilometres (220 square miles), which is roughly the size of London or San Francisco.

The Valley forms part of the midlands which lie between the Mahabharat range to the south and the Great Himalayan range to the north, at 85° 50' E and 27° 50' N. The alluvial floor of the Valley is at an altitude of between 1,200 and 1,500 metres (3,937 and 4,900 feet) above sea level and is subdivided by various watercourses, low ridges and hillocks. The temperature varies between 30°C (86°F) and freezing.

As the Valley is located in the subtropical zone and has good irrigation, it is very suitable for the cultivation of rice—the staple diet of the Nepalis—during the monsoon period, and wheat during the dry season.

Natural beauty is visible at every turn. From the capital, the snow-capped peaks of the Himalaya can be seen towering above the foothills encircling the Valley. In the Valley itself, the landscape is dramatically sculpted by the contours of the paddy fields. The towns and villages are alive with the colours of farm produce, ranging from pyramids of golden grain to the vivid reds of chilli peppers laid out on mats to dry in the sun. Throughout the countryside, vivid splashes of red and yellow flowers, poinsettia and marigold, and a host of others grown for votive offerings, augment this remarkable intensity of colour.

The foothills bordering the Valley were once heavily forested, but the density of these forests is now sadly depleted, leaving just a lace-like fringe along the upper reaches of the basin. Terraced fields of rice and maize slowly edge their way up the sides of the Valley.

The agricultural scene would be incomplete without the herds of goats, the droves of buffalo, the irascible Brahminy bull, and the ever-present sacred cow. The goats rush about scavenging purposefully, usually with a small child in hot pursuit who tries to call the herd to order. The buffaloes wallow in muddy pools under the watchful eye of a pretty girl, confront an unsuspecting visitor from their stable beneath the farmhouse, or round a sharp bend in the pathway. The bulls stand sentinel to nothing in particular, while the cows, aware of their immunity, stroll through the main streets and markets, blissfully oblivious to the bustle of activity around them, but always with a wary eye open for a chance to purloin an unguarded cabbage or bunch of carrots.

In the streets and towns there is a constant bustle of activity, especially in the bazaars and markets where the farmers sell their vegetables and fruit. The sacred cows wander around these makeshift stalls, scrounging fodder from unsuspecting stall-holders.

Added to this is the cacophony of the rickshaws and the intrusion of the motor vehicle whose propulsion is apparently activated by excessive use of the klaxon! Off the main street, in a network of smaller alleys and hemmed in by overhanging structures, goldsmiths and silversmiths fashion intricate patterns for jewellery. Perhaps a drumbeat or the discordant notes of a band will announce a religious festival, a wedding, or a family paying homage to their special deity with floral offerings and incense or butter-lamps. Here, deep within the fabric of the city and unaffected by the outside world, daily life goes on as it has for generations.

The People

Add to this setting the most colourful element—the people of the Valley. They are not all from the Valley, nor are they all like the old Sherpa lady and her clans; they are a sprinkling of people from the other 26 or more tribes of Nepal who flock to their capital in search of the proverbial streets paved in gold. The variety of ethnic groups to be encountered in Kathmandu, especially just before a major festival, can range from Bote tribes from the Nepali–Tibetan border, and Sherpas, Gurungs and Tamangs from the middle hills, to Rajputs, Majhis and Tharus from the lowlands of the Terai, and the Brahmins, Chhetris and Newars who inhabit the Valley itself. The women are all gaily dressed in brightly coloured saris and sparkling necklaces with brilliant flowers in their hair. The men are more restrained in their attire, usually wearing the traditional trousers—baggy at the top, tight round the calves—or a *lungi* (sarong) and cross-over shirt, with their Nepali cap or *topi* being their only concession to colour. The mountain people and Tibetans lend added variety to the characters who pass regularly through the Valley. Dressed in sheepskins and maroon upper garments to combat the cold weather, they are unkempt and often unwashed, but their striking features, twinkling eyes and smiling faces belie the harsh conditions they have to contend with.

Since space is restricted in most dwellings, a vast amount of human activity takes place in the open spaces—the squares, the temple forecourts and even along the streets. Grain is threshed and winnowed, clothes and children are washed, and babies are oiled, massaged and preened in the sunshine. All this with an almost total disregard for the traffic and the inconvenience to business that it might cause.

The backdrop for all this activity is the intricately carved temple façades and quaint terraced brick houses which add a warm red hue to the scene. While a flash of gold over the roofs denotes the finial of a religious structure, swathes of vegetables hanging from the roof indicate an active homestead below housing several generations.

As a visitor to Nepal you will probably base yourself in Kathmandu, the capital city, aptly located in the middle of the Valley. Following rapid development over the last 15 years, great changes have taken place in the city. In the main, this is only a façade, for behind is hidden a wealth of fascinating historic buildings and lingering traditions and customs.

Before embarking on your fact-finding tour, it is worth while experiencing the quite special atmosphere that pervades the Valley: the timelessness, the magical quality of the light and colour—especially at dawn and dusk—and the intangible and unrelated sense of urgency and bustle to be found in the busy streets and bazaars. Imbibing this atmosphere will contribute to your enjoyment of the more formal tours you might make during your stay in the Valley.

The Forms of Cities, Towns and Villages

Perhaps the most famous bazaar in Kathmandu is that of Asan Tol (see page 86). It occupies a road that runs diagonally from the Durbar Square (see pages 73–82), across the north–south and east–west-oriented streets of the city. It was probably an old trading and pilgrimage route linking Baudha with Swayambhu, the two major Buddhist centres in the Valley.

Along this street there used to be a mass of small, traditional shops built in the typical Newari style of terraced buildings behind which lie a myriad of passages, courtyards and shrines occupied by extended family groups. Here one finds the traders, businessmen and craftsmen in what at first appears to be a disorganized conglomeration but is actually a balanced society of mutually dependent groups. Sadly, this unique façade is being decimated by the demands of tourist development. They have either been camouflaged by the vendors' wares—carpets have replaced saris, plastic buckets have elbowed out brass pots—or worse still, sections of the old terraces have been torn down to be replaced by high-rise business premises or apartments which totally destroy the harmony of a street that only very recently was still intact.

If you can penetrate the superficial modernity, you will find that tradition still survives behind both the old and new fronts, as in each specialized area, or *tol*, crafts and businesses are carried on to service and support their outlet on the main street, whether it be brass and copper ware, candles, clothing or assembling the latest Chinese push-bike!

In the centre of Asan you can still find the place where rice is traded in large quantities, and where people from all over the Valley come to sell their crops or to buy their supplies. Many different varieties of rice are heaped up in front of the picturesque Annapurna Temple (see page 86) built in the early 19th century.

Branching off the main street you will find yourself in a network of smaller alleys. The deeper you penetrate into the maze of streets, the closer you will get to seeing ways of life that have persisted virtually unchanged over centuries—potters, metalworkers and blacksmiths working just as their forefathers did to turn out the same products. These first explorations are the

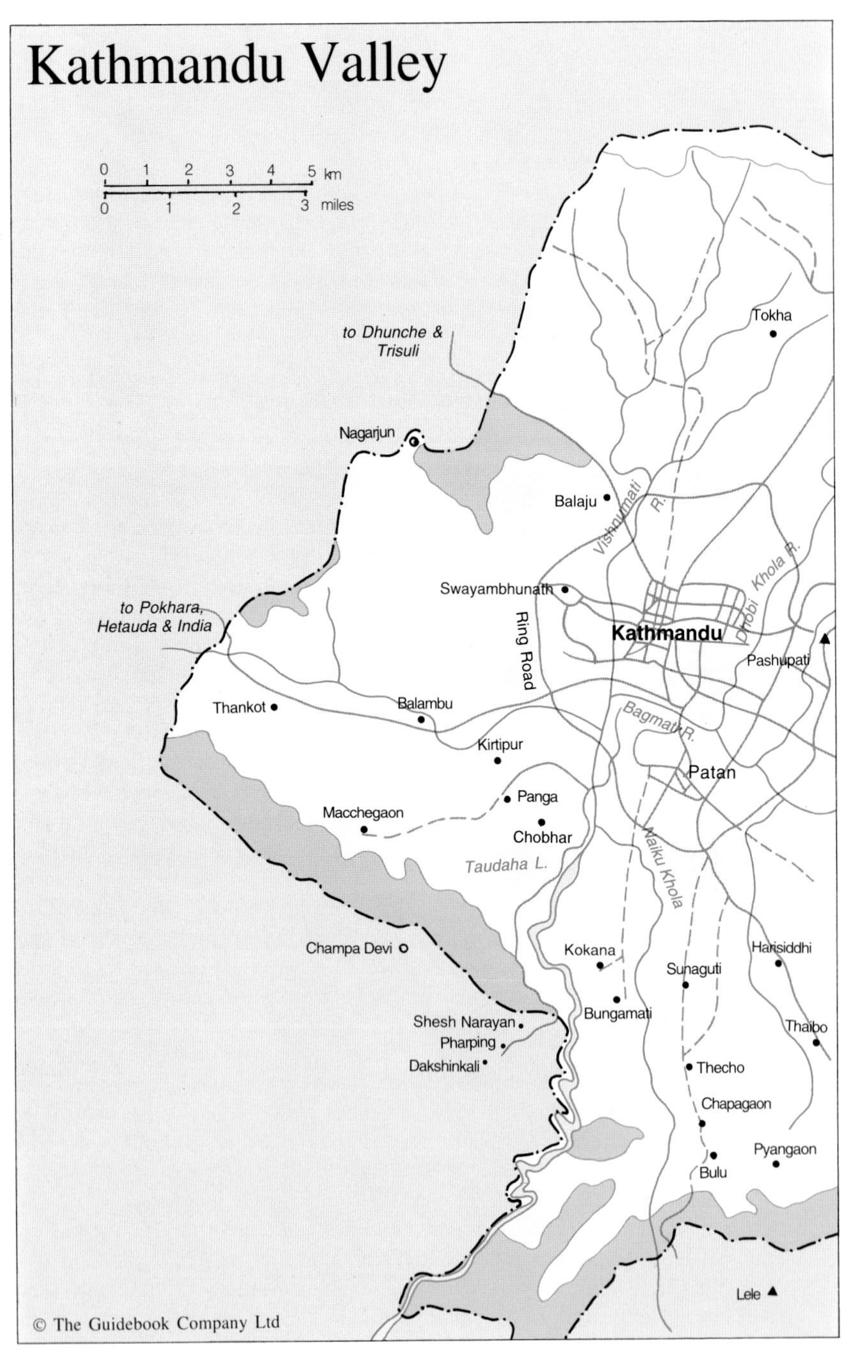
Kathmandu Valley
0 1 2 3 4 5 km
0 1 2 3 miles
to Dhunche & Trisuli
Tokha
Nagarjun
Balaju
Vishnumati R.
Dhobi Khola R.
Swayambhunath
to Pokhara, Hetauda & India
Ring Road
Kathmandu
Pashupati
Thankot
Balambu
Bagmati R.
Kirtipur
Patan
Panga
Macchegaon
Chobhar
Taudaha L.
Naiku Khola
Champa Devi
Kokana
Harisiddhi
Sunaguti
Bungamati
Shesh Narayan
Thaibo
Pharping
Dakshinkali
Thecho
Chapagaon
Pyangaon
Bulu
Lele

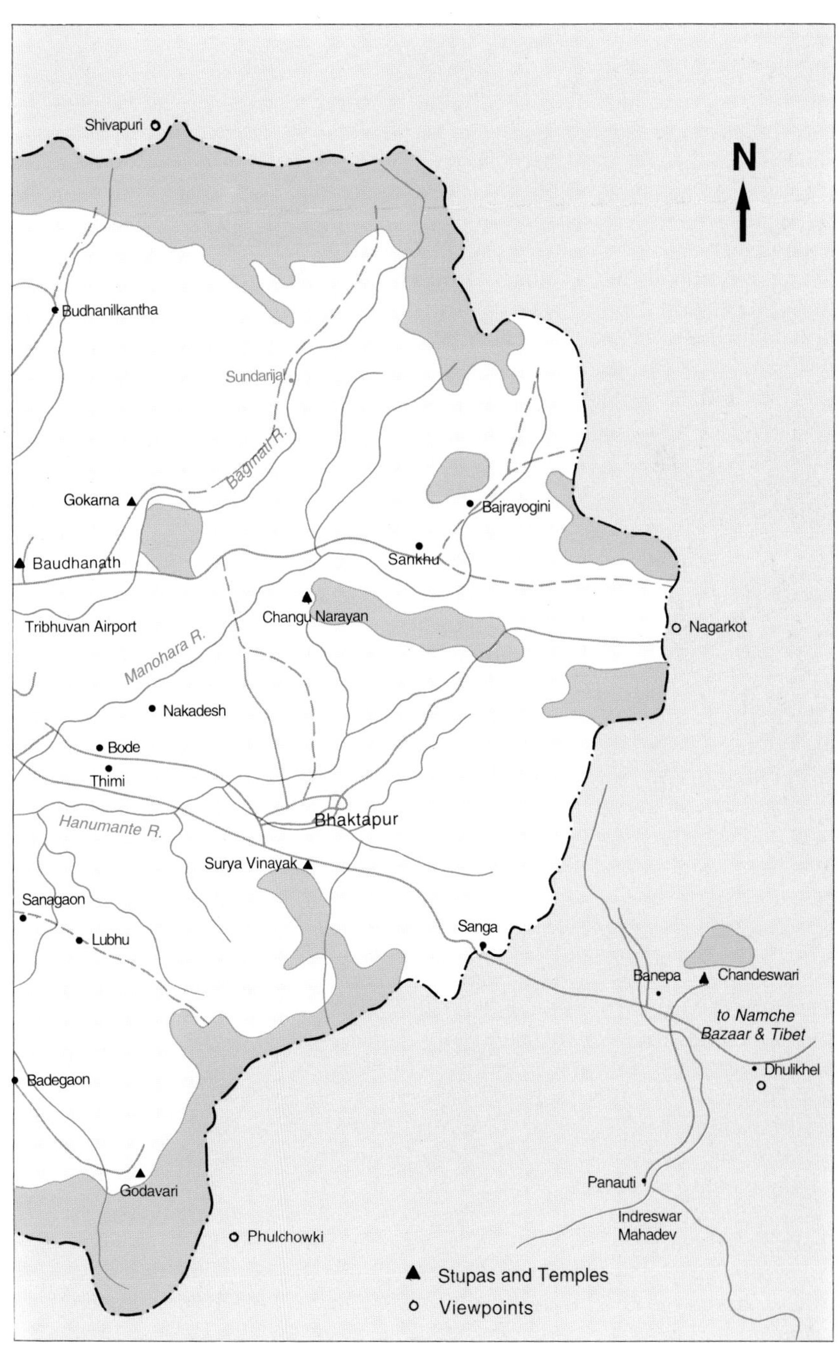

N
Shivapuri
Budhanilkantha
Sundarijal
Bagmati R.
Gokarna
Bajrayogini
Sankhu
Baudhanath
Changu Narayan
Tribhuvan Airport
Nagarkot
Manohara R.
Nakadesh
Bode
Thimi
Hanumante R.
Bhaktapur
Surya Vinayak
Sanagaon
Lubhu
Sanga
Banepa
Chandeswari
to Namche Bazaar & Tibet
Dhulikhel
Badegaon
Godavari
Panauti
Indreswar Mahadev
Phulchowki
Stupas and Temples
Viewpoints

ones you will remember most vividly and, probably more important, the ones that will make you more responsive to the wealth of experiences about to come your way in the days that follow.

Despite development, the towns and villages of the Kathmandu Valley have remained relatively unaltered in their concept, since lifestyles and building materials have changed only in the last quarter century. Roads linking one settlement to another follow the original trade routes across the farmland between them. To some extent the forms of the cities have been dictated by these road patterns rather than by the classical layouts described in Hindu mythology and classical Sanskrit texts. The roads have also encouraged towns to develop and grow considerably over the last decade, in some cases so that adjacent towns have merged, and former boundaries have dissolved.

Many towns and villages lie along the trade routes that crisscross the Valley. The age-old problem of defence, the importance of occupying the least amount of irrigated agricultural land, and the need for protection against floods, have led to many settlements being built on high ground in the vicinity of streams and rivers. In spite of the traditional belief that Bhaktapur, Patan and Kathmandu were originally laid out in the shapes of a conch shell, discus and sword respectively—the symbols of the deity Manjusri—it is far more likely that these towns and other villages, colonies and settlements have adopted forms and patterns suited to their topography, have been amalgamated, linked with new roads and surrounded by walls to form the towns we know today.

Kathmandu lies at the junction of two main trading routes: the north–south route running between Patan and the foothills of the Himalaya, which was the trade route to Tibet through Helambu and Langtang; and the more local route between Swayambhu and Baudha. Patan is quartered by two trade routes linking it with the other two cities, while Bhaktapur lies along a busy market street. Even though the durbar squares, with their palaces and important associated buildings, established the centres of power and culture, it was the market streets that gave the towns their alignment. In Bhaktapur, the main street is not the one normally taken to the durbar square, but that which branches off to the right at the outskirts of the western entry to the town and running parallel to it. The shapes of these cities were established long before the siting of the existing durbar squares, a fact that can easily be confirmed by tracing the routes of some of the religious processions that have followed the same route over several centuries. These processions use streets and alleyways that are quite distinct from the newly impressed pattern of both pedestrian and vehicular traffic.

The similarity in the development of streets and squares within the Valley's towns and cities is linked to the individual building types, such as private houses, monastic complexes and temples and shrines. These individual elements provide the terraces, courtyards and squares, which have themselves expanded and developed to form the town districts or *tols* by which localities are known. The streets of the old cities have no particular name; they are located by the *tol* they are in. The most frequently used *tol* names have their origin in those of the temples or monasteries around which they developed. Other *tols* got their names from the skills or trades of those who lived in them. Likewise, some of the smaller settlements which developed around a particular shrine or temple derived their names from the deity worshipped there.

Besides the three main cities in the Valley, there are several small towns and religious centres, most of which can offer the visitor something of interest, whether it be a historic building, a wonderful vista or a traditional craft.

To experience everything of value would take several years. Although the scope of this book is limited, the experiences it guides you to will remain with you long after you have forgotten the names and dates of the numerous historic buildings that you will see.

The History of the Valley

Over the past two thousand years the Kathmandu Valley has sheltered the dominating power of the central part of the Himalaya, the kingdom of Nepal. Whilst maintaining an independent existence, the Valley has exerted a major influence on the surrounding smaller states but, unlike them, the Valley has enjoyed a relatively continuous development despite the changes wrought by immigrants and marauders. A constant source of attraction to outsiders because of its location and its wealth of important Hindu and Buddhist shrines, it has always been one of the most important pilgrimage sites for Hindus in the central Himalaya.

The beginning of Nepal's history is still very much in the realm of myth and legend. It is popularly believed that the Kathmandu Valley was originally a lake—a fact substantiated by geological studies—which was drained by the supernatural intervention of Manjusri, a divinity worshipped by both Hindus and Buddhists. Thereafter, the Bodhisattva is reputed to have founded the first settlement in the Valley. Further traditions connect both the Buddha and the Mauryan emperor Ashoka with the Valley, claiming that Ashoka visited Nepal and was responsible for the erection of the four cardinal *stupas* in Patan. It is possible that his daughter visited Patan and was betrothed to one of the Malla kings. To date, little historical or archaeological evidence exists to support either legend.

It is only in the fifth and sixth centuries of the current era that the first facts and dates appear. These are recorded in inscriptions and the writings of Chinese explorers who give interesting accounts of the Kathmandu Valley, then ruled by the Licchavi Dynasty. The records of the Licchavis are more authentic than those of earlier dynasties. From the time of the Buddha, the Licchavis were known to have established a tribal republic on the northern Gangetic plain and it is probable that the rulers of the Kathmandu Valley came from this group, as they moved up from the plains around the second and third centuries AD. The earliest inscriptions are found at Changu Narayan and belong to the fifth century.

The next great contributors to the cultural heritage of Nepal were the rulers of the third Malla Dynasty, which was founded in 1350 by Jayastithi Malla. His reforming reign ushered in a high period of artistic and architectural activity, the products of which are still in evidence. Under the rule of the Mallas, a period of relative stability began which lasted almost 600 years. With the death of Jayastithi's grandson, Yaksha Malla, in 1482, the Valley was divided among his three sons and the kingdoms of Kantipur, Lalitpur and Bhaktapur, now the cities of Kathmandu, Patan and Bhadgaon, were established.

With the Valley thus divided, none of the three rulers was powerful enough to prevent the disintegration of his own territory. The kingdoms shrank to city states and disunity arose among the rulers. Paradoxically, disunity among the Valley kingdoms had an almost positive effect on their arts and architecture. Despite continuous skirmishes between these city states, a competitiveness in these fields developed which led to the construction of even more spectacular temples and palaces.

The divisions among the petty kingdoms of the Valley enabled a small kingdom in central Nepal, called Gorkha, to become the strongest power in the region. Through clever political manœuvring the Gorkha king, Prithvi Narayan Shah, brought about the downfall of the Mallas in 1763 and, with his conquest of the Valley, Nepal was finally unified. However, this only came about after a protracted ten-year campaign of siege and conquest of individual settlements which led finally to the capture of the three main cities.

About 80 years after the rise to power of Prithvi Narayan Shah, palace intrigues had increased to such an extent that in 1846 Jung Bahadur Rana, who had elevated himself to the position of prime minister, became *de facto* ruler of Nepal. This came about after a bloody massacre during a royal assembly at the Kot in which the majority of the ruling government was exterminated. (The exact buildings of the Kot no longer exist, but its location was in the vicinity of the Hanuman Dhoka Police Headquarters.) For the next 100 years the country was subjected to the rule of the Rana family which kept the country almost totally isolated from the outside world. Because the Ranas struck up a reasonable relationship with the British, they were able to travel not only to India but also to several European countries en route to Great Britain. This contact brought dramatic change in the style of building that took place. As a result of trading with nearby countries, the Arabian style of architecture came into vogue, but this was soon superseded by the extravagance of the neo-classical style prevalent in Britain and Europe at the time, which was imported on their return by the itinerant Ranas. This period, which disregarded the established traditional form of architecture and used local building materials, had a marked effect on the continuity of traditional building as well as influencing the craftsmen—the bricklayers, metalworkers and woodcarvers—responsible for manufacturing the materials.

It was only in 1951 that King Tribhuvan of the Shah dynasty, whose reign in exile began in 1911, sought political asylum in India. From there, one year later, he returned triumphantly to Nepal to oust the-then decadent Rana regime and to restore the sovereignty of the crown.

The partyless Panchayat System introduced by King Mahendra in 1960 kept the reins of power with a few élite people and was centred on the Royal Palace. For thirty years there was little opposition in any legal or parliamentary sense but the Nepali Congress Party and a few factions of the Nepal Communist Party continued to campaign against the Palace regime and for the restoration of democracy. However, in the last decade the political situation has changed dramatically. In January 1990 the many fractionalised opposition parties came together and supported the Nepali Congress programme of civil disobedience. Human Rights organizations throughout the world, and more significantly all India's political parties, supported the movement and in April the Panchayat System collapsed and the King appointed an interim government to draw up a new democratic constitution. With the country now a constitutional monarchy, in April 1991 the first fair and free elections were held and a Nepali Congress government was elected. However, the wide support for the Nepal Communist Party has continued to be a major nuisance for the new government, and Nepal still relies heavily upon foreign aid and expertise in its development programmes.

The traditional buildings that are mostly in evidence throughout the Valley today represent the craft and architecture of the Malla Dynasty, which started in the 14th century, survived the early Shah period, but faded rapidly during the Rana era.

For traditionalists, it is sad to see a unique environment which had spontaneously maintained a balance with nature engulfed by the modern materialist world. While the conservation of tradition and culture should not be allowed to stand in the way of modern development, it is equally important that development and the means adopted to achieve it should not be allowed to destroy the human values embedded in Nepal's unique life-style.

Religion

Perhaps one of the most difficult elements to grasp in the Nepali people's way of life is their religion and their religious practices. Their religious fervour is indeed intense and devout. Their religious practices, especially Hindu ones, follow a typical pattern of physical offering which is extremely colourful, as can be witnessed by the variety and abundance of festivals celebrated throughout the year (see page 167–75). When the uninitiated visitor attempts to understand something of the religions practised in the Valley, the number and variety of deities immediately apparent are indeed very confusing. 'There are as many gods as there are people and as many temples as there are dwellings in the Valley of Kathmandu' goes a saying. This is not far from the truth, as each dwelling has its own little shrine housing the family god in a room directly under the roof.

The two main religions in the Valley are Hinduism and Buddhism, the former being the religion of the crown, the king being considered a living incarnation of the god Vishnu. Both Hinduism and Buddhism have assimilated many elements of an indigenous shamanist religion based on a belief in supernatural beings, often personifications of natural phenomena, and in the ability of certain people, the shamans, to communicate with them.

Hinduism

Hindus have always believed that the totality of existence, including God, man and the universe, is too vast to be contained within a single set of beliefs. Their religion therefore embraces a wide variety of metaphysical systems or viewpoints, some mutually contradictory. From these, an individual may select one which is congenial to him, or conduct his worship simply on the level of family morality and observances.

Religious practices differ somewhat from group to group and the average Hindu does not need any systematic or formal creed in order to practise his religion; he need only comply with the practices of his family and social group. One basic concept in the Hindu religion is that of *dharma*, one's duty to follow the natural law and the social and religious obligations it imposes. It holds that every person should play his proper role in society, and the system of caste, although not essential to philosophical Hinduism, has become an integral part of its social expression. Under this system, each person is born into a particular caste whose traditional occupation—not necessarily practised—is graded according to the degree of purity or impurity inherent in it.

Other fundamental ideas common to nearly all Hindus concern the nature and destiny of the soul and the basic forces of the universe. *Karma* is the belief that the consequences of every good or bad action must be fully realized. Rebirth is required by *karma* in order that the consequences of action may be fulfilled. Thus the role an individual must play throughout his life is fixed by his good and evil actions in his previous existences. It is only when the individual soul sees beyond the veil of illusion—the force leading to the belief in appearance rather than the reality of things—that it is able to realize its identity with the impersonal, transcendental reality that is Brahma, and escape from the otherwise endless cycle of rebirth.

Although many of the high-caste families tend to conform to the Hinduism of the Brahmin priests and their religious texts, a majority of the people, especially among the lower castes, are much less orthodox in the gods they worship. The ordinary villager knows very little about the concept of the divine unity underlying all things, including the gods, and, as a result, his belief is in an impersonal force that controls fate.

Each village often has its own patron deities who can be related to the greater deities of the Hindu pantheon. However, more often these deities are personifications of natural phenomena. Much importance is given to shamanism and to the role of the all-embracing female divinity, Devi. While gods are usually believed to be responsible for protecting the village land and resources, goddesses are supposed to be responsible for the well-being of the group. In addition to village deities, there are other divinities, usually ancestral spirits, who are guardians of the safety of the family and who are worshipped generation after generation.

The majority of the deities are worshipped out of fear, for their power and wrath rather than for their love, and are believed to be very much involved in even the daily life of human beings. Religion is seen more as a means of placating and propitiating powerful supernatural beings of uncertain temper, rather than as being concerned with offering thanks and devotion to lovable and beneficent deities.

Hinduism has priests, but there is no ecclesiastic organization. There are temples, but there is no Church. The only authority is the Vedic scripts. The priests are from Brahmin castes and act as chaplains to families of the upper castes. The central religious act is public or private worship, the *puja*, which consists largely of welcoming the god to the company of its worshippers. If the *puja* is a public occasion, as one at a large public festival might be, the deity is ceremonially bathed and dressed, incensed, worshipped with fire, flowers and sweetmeats, and then paraded through the streets. At a private *puja*, simple offerings are made by a family or an individual within the household. For many worshippers, their idol is regarded and worshipped as the actual deity, but an idol is not essential to worship and a substitute icon can take its place.

In marked contrast to the quiet observance of most Buddhist festivals, Hindu festivals are far more actively celebrated as outward demonstrations of worship and religious fervour. Buddhist worship is more of a mental exercise than a physical activity.

Popular Gods in the Hindu Pantheon

The three main Hindu gods are Brahma, Vishnu and Shiva—the personifications of creative, preservative and destructive forces respectively. Almost all Hindus are followers of either Vishnu or Shiva, or one of their incarnations, and are known either as Vaishnavas or Shaivas. Vishnu is the preserver of life and his origins go back to the Vedic gods where he is identified with Narayan, whose wife is Lakshmi, the goddess of prosperity. The chief responsibility of Vishnu is to intervene from time to time to save the world from destruction. To do this he assumes corporeal forms such as Narasimha, the man-lion, Varaha, the boar, or Krishna, the ideal youth, lover and statesman, who is the most famous of the ten incarnations or *avatars* associated with Vishnu. Krishna is one of the more popular divinities in Nepal, with several important temples dedicated to him.

The Shaiva sect is the most common in Nepal but, due to either regional or clan differences, Shiva has become a more complex divinity, personifying the awesome and frightening aspects of faith. Shiva embodies the struggle against demons and evil, the potential dangers of knowledge and the fact of death and deterioration. He is the destroyer and regenerator, a god of a thousand aspects, names and manifestations, but unlike Vishnu, Shiva has very few incarnations. Shiva has traditionally been the god of the ascetics, the scantily clad, long-haired and ash-covered, trident-bearing itinerant religious beggars present at most festivals. Considered to be the supreme being, Shiva has also creative and benevolent aspects, appearing often under both male and female guises. Seen as the mother goddess, Shiva has two aspects—one beneficent as the goddess Uma, and the other more often stern and frightening, as the goddesses Durga and Kali. In his other common, fierce form, as Bhairab, he is seen as a multi-armed, demon-like creature with fierce, staring eyes and fangs and wearing a garland of skulls. In the aspect of rebirth and regeneration, Shiva is represented by a phallic symbol (*lingam*), which is found often in combination with a *yoni*, a plate-like, rimmed disc, being the female symbol on which the *lingam* stands. The significance of the sexual symbolism lies in the fact that the male element is conceived of as the passive motionless centre of the wheel of existence and the female element as the energy which revolves around it. In the unity of the two is perfect bliss, perfect wisdom and perfect consciousness.

Perhaps one of Shiva's most venerated forms is in his own guise as Pashupati, the lord of animals and protector of the Valley. The deity Pashupati is unique to Nepal, and the temple at Pashupatinath is a great centre of pilgrimage.

Ganesh, the benevolent elephant god and master of Shiva's troupe, is a very popular and much-worshipped divinity in Nepal. He is the son of Shiva and Parvati, the problem-solver and remover of obstacles, in addition to being the god of wealth. Before any major undertaking or journey, Ganesh must be consulted and his shrines visited, especially the small shrine near the Kasthamandap in Kathmandu where travellers make offerings to ensure a safe journey.

Buddhism

Buddhism had its origins in the teachings of Siddhartha Gautama, who was born about 553 BC in Lumbini, which is 250 kilometres (155 miles) south-west of Kathmandu, in the Nepali Terai. At the age of 29, he renounced family and home and spent six years in meditation, until he attained enlightenment. Thereafter known as the Buddha, the Enlightened One, he devoted the rest of his life to preaching his doctrine. He accepted or reinterpreted the basic concepts of Hinduism and was intent on restoring a concern with morality to religious life, a concern that has been stifled in a mass of ritual details and external observances.

Gautama promulgated the four noble truths: suffering dominates life; desire causes suffering; desire comes to an end in *nirvana*; *nirvana*, perfect bliss arising out of extinction of self and absorption into supreme spirit, can be achieved by the eightfold path. This path to *nirvana* is an individual struggle and results in the passing over of the individual self into the eternal self. Individual morality is the means of gaining *nirvana*, not the observance of caste or priestly rituals. While the concept of the union of the individual with the void as the end of existence is common to Hinduism and Buddhism, they differ on the means of achievement. Buddhist devotees have naturally been very much influenced by their contacts with their Hindu counterparts and there is a sense of unity between the two religions, even to the extent that both religions often use the same temples and worship the same divinities. As Tantrism developed, the Buddhist community adopted many Hindu ideas and gods. Buddhism was probably reintroduced into Nepal by Ashoka, who annexed at least part of the country to his empire, and it was through Nepal that Buddhism first entered Tibet.

The two main forms of Buddhism are those of Hinayana, which is the earliest form, and Mahayana, which developed at about the beginning of the Christian era and was based more on the example of the Buddha than on his specific statements. Buddhism in Nepal took on a new dimension with the creation of Vajrayana Buddhism, an offshoot of Mahayana. It was most widely practised by the Newars in the Kathmandu Valley. The meaning of Vajrayana is 'Path of the Thunderbolt', the thunderbolt or Vajra becoming the main ritual object for the Buddhist monks. It is here that the philosophical thought of Hinduism and Buddhism is very similar. Vajrayana departs from Mahayana in its emphasis on Tantric religious symbolism, but the two forms do not differ in their basic beliefs. To the Vajrayana belongs the conception of the five Dhyani Buddhas with their corresponding Dhyani Bodhisattvas, aspects of which appear in meditation on the one, primordial Adi-Buddha.

Tantrism

All religions in Nepal, whether Hindu or Buddhist, are strongly influenced by the Tantric cult which infiltrated Nepal from India. The term 'Tantrism' is drawn from an analogy with warp and weft in weaving—the warp of Buddhist philosophy being interwoven with meritorious action. In its mediaeval growth, Tantrism expanded the realm of the Hindu divinities and their cults and rites, adding a new element to their activities. The numerous Tantric deities come in a variety of multiple-limbed forms symbolizing the omnipotence of the divine. In contrast to Buddhism, Tantrism substituted concrete action and direct experience for contemplative meditation. It soon degenerated into obscure practices, often of a sexual nature, purportedly to reach beyond one's own limitations to attain perfect and divine bliss. In theory, Tantrism is an attempt to synthesize spiritualism with materialism, where practitioners seek to expand their mental faculties by mastering the forces of nature to achieve peace of mind.

PHILIPS

CONCERN

Building Styles

Perhaps the most remarkable aspect of the Nepali cultural heritage is the limited area in which it is prevalent. A few temples in the traditional Nepali style have been built in the larger provincial settlements of central Nepal and an occasional example of a copy, the result of the whim of some rich merchant, can be discovered in the foothills of the Himalaya, but the major area of Nepal's true history and culture lies within the Kathmandu Valley. Nowadays, the exquisite craft of Nepali woodcarving is recognized far beyond the confines of the Valley, even beyond Nepal, but the Valley is its source and its home. When one speaks of Nepali culture, especially of artistry and craftsmanship, it is in the early stages almost exclusively a Newari culture.

Only a few buildings survive from the early years of Nepal's history. These are all either in ruin or consist of *stupas*, memorials to holy men. They are solid structures and mostly of archaeological rather than architectural interest.

The culture still extant in the Kathmandu Valley is the product of much later history, as late as the 17th century, and is abundantly in evidence in the form of the traditional Newari temples and palaces. However, there are many surviving ruins of earlier buildings now incorporated in newer ones, earlier doors and windows or pillars supporting roof struts (*tunasi*), which can often be dated by inscriptions. There are a few inscribed stones of very early periods, but they can no longer be related to the buildings as they are seen today. Nepal gives the impression of being a remarkable survival from the Indian Middle Ages; in fact, its buildings are seldom as old as the mediaeval period of Europe. The impression may not be so false, as it seems certain that the 17th-century builders were deliberately perpetuating earlier styles, just as the craftsmen were striving to produce earlier forms of art.

Most travel and history books refer to the temples as being multi-*storeyed* rather than as having multi-*tiered* roofs. More often than not, the roofs do not correspond with the floor levels, if in fact there are any definable floor levels as such in a temple. Such a differentiation is very important, as most of the temples comprise mainly a sanctuary cell on the ground floor, over which there is intentionally unoccupied space. In the case of only a very few temples, where the shrine containing the deity occupies an upper floor, is there more than one floor. The concept of the temple, as opposed to the small shrine, follows the basic ideal of any religious building: to construct, as an act of worship and dedication to a god, the finest building that the worshippers are capable of producing. The sense of greatness is nearly always achieved by height and the qualities of proportion and perspective are something very special to this style. There is, however, one great difference that must be kept in mind when comparing the Nepali temple to the Christian church or the

Muslim mosque. The latter two are designed to accommodate large congregations gathered for corporate worship, whereas the former is intended for private, individual worship—the *puja*. The sanctuary, often not much more than a mere square metre (seven square feet), houses the image of the deity only. The *puja* enables private communion between the worshipper and the god under cover of the projecting roof. Even during large family festivals, when the leader has performed the necessary rites for the whole gathering, individual worship follows. Large public festivals are held in open spaces around the temples where numerous resthouses, or *pathis*, of all shapes and sizes provide the necessary shelter for the pilgrims.

Concern for periods and datable styles may, in the case of Nepali architecture, become irrelevant because here the art is expressed in a traditional form as opposed to an individual form. Its vitality consists not in the development of personal expression, but in the perpetuation of what is traditionally correct. Of course, there is a form of development and this can be seen in the way that traditional craftsmen are progressing today when faced with problems of repairing a former building. But such progress is obviously slow and incidental, while the main forms have remained unchanged for centuries. Thus, while marked variations in quality and decoration can be discerned in the woodcarving and the standard building details, it is probable that the actual building styles have undergone little change. More marked changes in traditions took place with the advent of the first major Western influence during Rana rule.

There are certain styles of architecture that are easily recognizable and which can be roughly dated by centuries. Unlike European architecture, there appears to have been little development in Nepali building styles. There are purely local variations in the type of decoration and they are usually dictated by the divinity housed within the structure.

The Traditional Newari Style

The most interesting, and most prolific, form of Newari architecture is the brick-built temple with diminishing-tiered roofs. It seems to be generally agreed now that it is the survival of an ancient Indian style, long since abandoned in its land of origin. The survival of this style in certain remote areas of India, and the descriptions by Chinese pilgrims of Indian temples over a thousand years ago, confirms this. Fortunately, it is not just the building as a type that survives in Nepal, but a whole style of architecture which, although it may owe much to India, now exists as something distinctly Nepali.

Nepali temples are all based on the same concept, but differ in shape and size. To achieve the sense of height and majesty, they are mostly set on diminishing-stepped plinths. They are built of brick—often special glazed

Traditional Temple

brick—with carved timbers supporting the heavy pitched roof construction. The roofs are covered with tiles bedded in a clay base. The top roof is capped with a pinnacle (*gajur*), which is often very ornate and, on some of the more important temples, made of gilded copper. A temple may be free-standing or attached to a terrace of houses. It can be square, rectangular, or even octagonal in plan, and its size could be anything from a small two-square-metre (15-square-foot) structure to something the size of the Taleju Temple in Kathmandu, which is well over 33.5 metres (110 feet) high and occupies the central place in a large courtyard. There appears to be no guiding principle concerning the number of roof tiers. Most temples have three; the smaller ones, mostly attendant shrines, have only two. Temples dedicated to Pashupati, which are often of sizeable proportions, always have two large projecting roofs. There are only two free-standing temples with five-tiered roofs: the Nyatapola Temple (see page 125) in Bhaktapur and the Kumbheswar Temple (see page 111) in Patan.

The Shikhara

Another striking building style that has become fairly common over the last two centuries is the *shikhara*, a brick or stone temple of geometrical form with a tall central spire rising to the heavens, suggesting the peaks of the

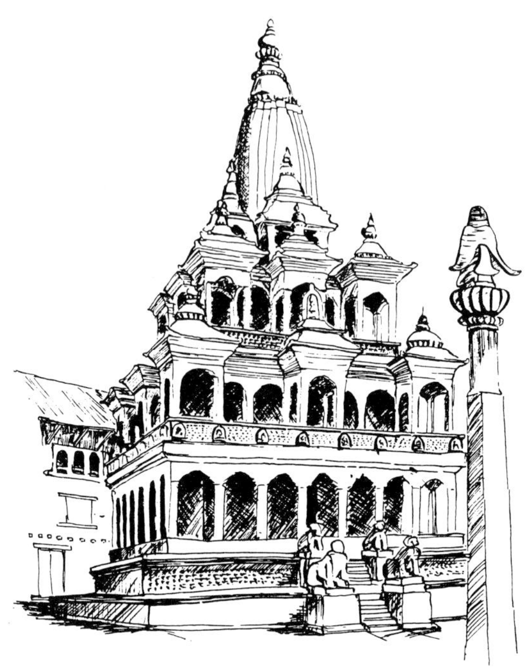

Shikhara

surrounding mountains. On each of the four elevations, and usually set above a colonnaded arcade, are attached porticoes which are said to symbolize the entrances to rock caves. Like most other religious buildings, the *shikhara* is set on a diminishing-stepped plinth and built around a small sanctuary containing the deity. The structure, usually symmetrical in form with a spire of solid construction, is capped with a pinnacle, often of gilded copper. As good building stone is not generally available in the Valley, most of the stone structures there have been sponsored by royalty and are generally found only in the durbar squares. The stone-built *shikharas* are therefore generally of rather special quality. One *shikhara* of particular note, the Mahabaudha in Patan (see page 112), is actually constructed in terracotta.

The *shikhara* is the typical building style of most Hindu shrines in India and it entered Nepal as a style only in the 17th century. Many Nepali shrines are, in fact, direct copies of famous Indian shrines.

The Stupa and Chaitya

The major *stupas* are dedicated exclusively to Lord Buddha and are solid hemispherical structures enshrining a relic of the Buddha, whether it be his mortal remains, as in the case of the *stupa* at Swayambhu, or some of his belongings, such as his garments or personal effects. The smaller *stupas*, or *chaityas*, as they are known, usually contain texts of prayers (*mantras*), holy scripts or, more especially in the hill areas, the mortal remains of an important and holy lama.

The *stupas* vary greatly in size, from the massive structure at Baudhanath to a variety of smaller versions that are scattered throughout Patan. The smaller *stupas* and *chaityas* are to be found in towns where Buddhists predominate. Their style of construction is basically uniform: the hemispherical mound is either made-up ground or a small hillock or rocky outcrop from which, as is the case at Swayambhu, the mound is formed. According to tradition, this mound of earth often covers a series of small *chaityas* grouped around a central one. Centrally placed on the mound is a small square structure (*chaku*) which supports the elaborate, usually gilded, pinnacle of 13 stages, on the base of which are the features unique to Nepal—the far-seeing eyes of the Buddha surveying the cardinal points. The third-century Ashoka *stupas* of Patan (see page 102) are much simpler in form and have only a plain brick *chaku*. The mounds of the later *stupas* are generally covered with brick or lime-concrete and whitewashed. During the major Buddhist festivals

Buddhist Stupa

Newari House

the dome is decorated with yellow clay poured over the whitewashed dome to make it resemble the lotus flower.

The Traditional Newari House

The development of urban settlements and of the street patterns within these has usually meant that dwellings are formed either around groups of interlocking courtyards in the more dense areas, or of terraced lines of houses facing onto a street or thoroughfare. In the latter case, a less controlled form of courtyard development—inferior structures interlocked by a series of enclosed passages at ground level—may take place. These may run beneath the dwellings and link the various courtyards. The buildings that overlook the main thoroughfares and those that occupy key positions in large enclosed spaces are usually of architectural importance. The façades are generally symmetrical and contain finely detailed and carved windows and doors. Symmetry is achieved on a central axis on each succeeding floor, with the central window of each floor emphasized by its size and quality of detail. The houses usually have two or three storeys above a ground floor and there is seldom any order to the placing of individual units in either quality or size—the symmetry exists only relative to an individual building. Where the ground floor is not used as a shop front or a workshop, the lower part of the elevation remains simple and unadorned, with a low door flanked by two small windows on either side. Irregularities that may occur at this level are never reported in the more formal layout of the upper storeys. Externally, the living area is marked by a special window consisting of either three or five bays. These windows can be of two different but standard patterns: a canted projecting bay of windows, or a projecting but vertical bay of windows. The bays may consist of units of odd numbers (three or five) and, on the more important buildings, these two standard patterns are combined vertically to form a very impressive and imposing central axis for the building.

Formerly, the typical window style was horizontal with squared latticework. Only 200 years ago, window designs started to change and to become more vertical in form, but they still retained the latticework. At the turn of this century, the trend was towards lighter and larger windows, latticework was omitted, and iron railings and shutters were introduced to close the now predominantly vertical style of window. Particular utilization of the rooms is decided by their vertical orientation and is not dependent on room size. Despite variations in size and external decoration, common principles of space utilization developed in all social groups. A central spine wall normally divides the ground floor into two narrow rooms, the front half overlooking the street usually serving as a shop or workshop, the rear portion as a place for storage. Living and sleeping quarters begin on the first floor and the location of specific functions is dictated by the size of the house and the number of families using it, as married sons by tradition take up residence with their families in their parental home.

In the common three-storeyed house, the second floor is the main living and family area. The spine wall is replaced by a row of twin columns forming a large, well-ventilated, low hall-like room suitable for family gatherings. On the exterior, large and finely carved windows emphasize the position of this living area. Both the kitchen and the family shrine are located in the attic space. Because of their religious significance, strangers and members of lower castes are banned from entering the kitchens or shrines of higher-caste dwellings.

Vihara: the Buddhist Monastery

The various types of Buddhist monastery in the Kathmandu Valley—as opposed to monastic buildings of the northern regions—are called *viharas*. This term encompasses basically two styles, the *bahil* and the *bahal*. The *bahil*, set on a raised platform above street level, is a two-storeyed structure surrounding an enclosed square courtyard. Except for the main entrance, consisting of a small, centrally-placed doorway flanked by two blind windows in the main elevation, the ground floor is totally sealed off from the outside. Arcaded porticoes on all four elevations overlook the internal yard. Directly opposite the main entrance is the free-standing shrine, with a clearly

Bahal

defined passageway around it. The shrine itself is a small, dark and simple rectangular room containing the image. To the left of the entrance there is a stone staircase leading to the upper floor. Over the main entrance, a projecting window forms the central axis to the main façade.

The *bahal* is again a two-storeyed building enclosing a courtyard, but unlike the *bahil*, its floor areas on both ground and upper floors are subdivided into several room-units. The building is generally of a more robust construction, set on a low plinth and overlooking a sunken square courtyard. The main entrance door, flanked on either side by windows, leads into a foyer with benches. As before, the main shrine is situated directly opposite this entrance and consists of a large, enclosed room containing the main divinity. The two flanking internal wings contain an open hall, similar to the entrance foyer, overlooking the courtyard. Set in the four corners of the building are stairways to the upper floor, each with a separate doorway leading from the courtyard. Each of the narrow stairways leads to a group of three rooms which form a separate unit with no intercommunicating doors or passages.

Perfect symmetry is achieved in *bahals* by generally projecting the central and corner sections of the brickwork on all façades and by the placement of windows and doors on a central axis. Each window is designed according to its location in the façade style. Although constructed of unglazed brick, the quality of the brickwork is excellent and is usually left exposed on the external façades. The interior façades are, however, usually rendered with a mud plaster and whitewashed. The entrance to the *bahal* and to the main shrine is indicated by a highly carved wooden tympanum or *torana*.

Math: the Hindu Priest House

The Nepali Hindu form of priest house is clearly distinct from the monastic buildings of Buddhism. First, it is not bound by such specific rules and, secondly, its location, orientation and internal planning correspond closely to that of a typical lay dwelling. The larger *math* generally comprises several smaller house-units ringed around a courtyard. It is usually a three-storeyed building of solid construction, with elevations resembling those of a residential house. It is fully integrated into a terrace of houses along a street or overlooking a square and may only be recognized by the superior quality of its decoration.

The variety and number of courtyards may differ and their particular uses are governed by their size and quality. However, utilization of space on the different floor-levels is essentially similar to that of the ordinary domestic dwelling. The ground floor serves as stables, stores, servants' quarters and guardrooms and there are usually shrines dedicated to Shiva and a *puja* room. The first and second floors contain living-rooms, guest-rooms and sleeping quarters, while the third floor contains the private shrine and the kitchen area. The exterior façades and the most important courtyard facades are usually faced with high-quality glazed bricks and the windows are heavily carved, as are the cornices and the brick lintels over the windows. The interior walls are generally of good-quality plain brickwork. The public areas, such as the stables, meeting-places, and so on, are paved with clay tiles, while the shrines are paved with stone slabs. The more domestic rooms have simple mud floors. Occasionally, the rooms occupied by the chief priest are more ornately decorated than the rest, with painted panels adorning the walls. The internal walls are otherwise plastered with mud and whitewashed.

Dharmashala: the Public Resthouse

A building type common to all towns and villages is the *dharmashala* or public resthouse, a place where travellers or pilgrims may rest free of charge. In Nepal these resthouses can range from the simple *pathi*, a small shelter usually at the intersection of important routes, to the more impressive buildings attached to or surrounding an important temple or shrine, or the *mandapa* which formerly served as the town assembly hall. These public resthouses were generally donated by wealthy individuals, religious groups or families, who were also responsible for their upkeep and maintenance.

The smallest of the group is the *pathi*, a small, raised and covered platform, which is either free-standing or incorporated into a dwelling. The

Pathi

layout of each *pathi* is almost identical and consists of a rectangular brick platform covered with wooden floorboards. As it is sited to overlook the access routes, the front is always open and of simple post and lintel construction.

Sattal is a general term for the more compound-type of public building. Unlike the *pathi*, the *sattal* seems to have been built not only for the transient traveller but also for longer sojourns by members of religious communities. Idols and shrines erected in *sattals* are, for the most part, features of later origin as they were seldom included in the original concept of the structure.

A two-storeyed pathi-type of *sattal* is commonly found in the durbar squares and might originally have quartered a part of the palace guard or other military unit. In such cases, the building is a little longer than is otherwise expected. The typical two-storeyed unit consists of a simple rectangular platform with a small door at the rear leading into the shrine. Otherwise, like the *pathi*, it is open on three sides. The upper floor is reached by an external stairway at the back of the *sattal*. This upper floor area is extended by cantilevering the floor over the front and side walls. On the upper floor there is another shrine, usually housing a private divinity and placed directly above the shrine below.

A *mandapa* is a square, single or multi-storeyed building which serves many functions similar to those of a *pathi*, yet it is mainly designed to be used as a community or reception hall. It is generally a free-standing open pavilion, facilitating large gatherings of people in or around it. It is always found within settlements and has its own particular importance. Unlike the simple *pathi*, this type is open on all sides. The roof is supported by an outer ring of pillars and a further four central pillars. In some cases, a further upper floor is constructed with a separate roof, following the typical temple structure. This upper floor is only accessible through a small hatch in the ceiling of the lower floor, and is used during festivals for the exposition of divinities, such as Indra during the festival of Indrajatra. For this reason there are canted, open balcony windows on all four sides. The sizes of *mandapas* vary considerably according to the size of the town or settlement they are serving, hence the Kasthamandap (see pages 81–2) in the centre of Kathmandu is, as can be expected, the largest to be found.

The Traditional Palace

All the palaces in the Kathmandu Valley are recognizable for their extravagant style and, in the major cities, for their scale and complexity. The relative proportions of these buildings are always much bigger than the general domestic scale; not only are the rooms larger, but all the elements appear larger and more splendid as these palaces were doubtless prestige buildings and often constructed in competition with the rival petty kingdoms in the Valley. The palaces exhibit perhaps the best examples of their period of

Palace in Durbar

Rana Palace

architecture, since the local craftsmen were encouraged to produce the finest quality of workmanship in recognition of their patrons and sponsors. The palaces are solidly built, not as fortresses as would be expected, but as examples of artistic and architectural beauty. They incorporate the qualities of religious architecture as well as those of monastic and domestic architecture.

The Rana Palace

Perhaps the only major and dramatic change in the styles of architecture in Nepal can be seen in the relatively recent arrival of the over-lifesize white stucco palaces introduced by the former Rana prime ministers (also see pages 88–9). This style is barely recognized today for its unique contribution to Nepal's architecture. Most of these palaces, which are of colossal proportions if compared to the style of architecture prevailing when they first appeared, and boast several hundred rooms, scores of courtyards and buildings scattered throughout the compounds, were built in a couple of years. The materials used were all available locally—bricks, mud mortar, timber and floor tiles. Only the 'new' style of interlocking roof tiles had to be imported and even these were soon manufactured in the Valley. The external decorative stucco work was executed in the local clays, copying the intricate designs at that time popular in Europe. The interiors were lavishly furnished with reproduction period furniture and decorated with exquisite crystal chandeliers and

mirrors, all conforming to the elaborate neo-classical revival that was taking place in Europe at the time. This colossal style of building had never been experienced before and, as a result, some of the finer points of both structural and detailed design suffered.

The interiors were laid out on a grand scale, with large state rooms, extensive family accommodation and vast areas of cramped living quarters for the family retinue and staff. Undoubtedly, the palaces were pretentious status-symbols and, although they were basically of identical construction, varied in both scale and decoration.

These extraordinary palaces now represent in Nepal a politically unstable period in the country's history; nevertheless, they also stand as a unique example of a style of architecture and an important period in the development of the towns and cities of the Kathmandu Valley.

Building Crafts and Craftsmen

The Hanuman Dhoka Conservation Project was the first major conservation programme to be undertaken by the Department of Archaeology of His Majesty's Government of Nepal in collaboration with UNESCO and the United Nations Development Programme (UNDP). This project, which was set up initially to conserve perhaps the most important historic structure in the Kathmandu Valley, the Hanuman Dhoka (see page 63), became the focal point for the conservation movement in Nepal as it was here that the crafts were revived, craftsmen were trained and conservation techniques evolved which became standard practice in the kingdom. The traditional family guilds of craftsmen were revived and fostered and such crafts as carving, traditional carpentry, brickmaking and metalwork are now skills much sought after. The rediscovery of such skills formed one of the many fascinating activities in the Hanuman Dhoka Conservation Project. In undertaking a major restoration programme, it was necessary to rely on traditional materials and craftsmen.

Woodcarving

Perhaps the best-known craft in Nepal is the woodcarving that adorns both domestic and religious buildings. This craft developed among the Newari tribes in the 15th and 16th centuries, during Malla rule. Today, it is still maintained by these same family guilds. However, the demand from commercial enterprises gives them little opportunity to practise their art form.

The Kathmandu Valley is the main stronghold of Nepali culture. The royal palaces of the Valley promoted the local arts and the best examples of each period of Nepali art are found in the buildings which comprise these palace ensembles.

Windows and floors are provided with a series of unique surrounds and mouldings. Cornices are built up of basic shapes which are derived from heads, birds or vegetal motifs. Each of these is a unique individual element.

The Vilas Mandir (see pages 70–3) of the Hanuman Dhoka Conservation Project contains some of the finest examples of technique and artistry in its woodcarving. The lower struts of the Basantapur Tower (see pages 71–2) are also particularly fine, as are the windows of both buildings. The grillwork of these windows is composed of a very complicated geometric, interlocking construction. Over 15 patterns have been discovered in this group of buildings alone, as well as several simpler forms. Unfortunately, these windows have deteriorated badly with time, damage by the monsoon rains, and distortion and loss due to earthquakes. They have also been heavily overpainted in an effort to overcome their tawdry appearance. The Hanuman Dhoka Project was faced not only with problems of replacement and repair, but also with the careful cleaning and conservation of the remaining examples of this disappearing art form.

Among other aims set out in the proposals of the project were the revival of interest in woodcarving and the setting up of local or family woodcarving guilds. As a long-term policy, these guilds would maintain the original woodcarving tradition and ensure a supply of skilled and willing craftsmen for conservation as well as increase the income of these families.

In the project's early stages, strong efforts were made to discover woodcarvers, as the general opinion held at that time was that few if any reliable and skilled artisans were left. The future of conservation in Nepal seemed dismal in the absence of traditional expertise. Fortunately, a reliable and competent team of traditional woodcarvers was discovered and up to 40 at one time were employed in the Hanuman Dhoka project.

As they worked, these artisans began to relive the spirit of their traditional craft and their work became part of their religion. There was a strict control of the type of work each man could perform, based upon his experience and competence. The task of 'opening' or carving the eyes of an image of a god could be carried out by only three men in Bhaktapur, an honour handed down from generation to generation, which is passed on to the next man only after certain religious rites have been performed.

Woodcarving was, until its recent revival, a dying tradition in Nepal and the men employed in the conservation project reported that they had previously been able to practise their craft for only one month a year. Most of these artisans worked with the project for its duration and their work improved rapidly. Their application was admirable, even though many of them had to travel 11 kilometres (seven miles) to work each day.

Working in close collaboration with the carvers was a large restoration section consisting of a team of over 50 young girls. All the original carved woodwork and brickwork was heavily encrusted with paint which needed to be removed. Under the direction of the Conservation Laboratory, part of the conservation project, the girls were trained in the processes of cleaning the woodcarvings. Originally it seemed that all the work would have to be executed *in situ*, but it was soon discovered that the majority of the carved timber windows and struts could be safely removed and cleaned more conveniently away from the building. The problem of dismantling, cleaning and replacing each piece of carving in its precise original position was overcome by the simple but effective method of numbering and recording each piece. Every piece of carving, of which there must have been over 20,000, was referenced against drawings. Each piece kept its number throughout its cleaning, repairing and chemical treatment. The number was removed only when it had been replaced and checked against the original on the drawings. In this way, the principles of conservation were faithfully followed and there was no falsification of historical evidence.

All the carvings had been painted and, in many cases, there was evidence of up to eight layers of colour on the carvings. After initial cleaning experiments, and when a nineteenth-century building was dismantled, revealing that the original carvings were unpainted, it was agreed that the carving should not be repainted.

Brickwork

The brickwork was also heavily painted, covering the original glaze. It was only after examining the building closely that paint was discovered to have been used to achieve unifying effects in buildings which were constructed in several phases and with different qualities of brickwork. Fortunately, the paint was mostly a distemper or water paint and could easily be removed by washing. Even so, the building had to be washed from its top to the ground.

The rediscovery of the method of making the original *telia* brick used in the Malla building era was a considerable achievement as the technique had been lost with the arrival of the new building styles. This special wedge-shaped brick, which has a thicker vertical face than back, was specially cut with a sharp scimitar-like blade to its unusual shape, glazed with a specially matured clay and burnished with a hematite stone—a gift from the gods!

During the conservation project in the Hanuman Dhoka and, subsequently, in several other projects, it was necessary to replace many unglazed or defective bricks with the traditional *telia* bricks. The rediscovery of the technique of making them was thus vital to the success of the future repair and conservation of historical monuments.

The fact that the brick is called *telia*, which means 'oiled', led the project team astray during their first experiments. No practical information about its manufacture had been found and direct experimentation had to be undertaken. These initial efforts were made in the traditional brick fields and, although it was unlikely that a brick resembling in any way the original model could be produced, a large crowd gathered to watch the mud-covered experimenters. Much to the enjoyment of the onlookers, an old man from the

back of the crowd called out that things were being done in the wrong way and went off to collect his tools, promising to return and demonstrate the correct way. A second old man disagreed with the procedure proposed by the first. The arguments between the two men eventually led to a compromise and the bricks were made and then fired. The results stood up almost perfectly to several comparative tests with the original bricks. Many varieties of brick were made and in each case the wedge shape was preserved.

Metalcasting

A craft that was by no means endangered but which brought a great element of fascination to the project was that of bell-casting. The method of casting metal objects using the *cire perdue*, or 'lost wax', process is still widely used in the Kathmandu Valley and the problem of producing new bells to hang from the rafter ends did not pose a great problem. However, the fact that each bell had to be given individual attention was somewhat daunting, especially as there were over 1,600 needed for the Basantapur Tower alone.

Each bell was made in the following way. The first step is the making of a wax model which is initially coated with a very fine-textured clay mixed with dung to a porridge-like consistency. The model is allowed to dry slowly, after which a second and perhaps a third layer of the same mixture is applied and dried. After this, a much coarser clay-mix is prepared by adding rice husks to act as a bonding agent, and this is applied over the model. By this time, each wax model has an outer coating about eight millimetres (a quarter of an inch) thick, which is carefully moulded over the model by hand. The mould thus formed is dried (away from sunlight) for several weeks, until an experienced bell-caster certifies that it is sufficiently dry to withstand molten metal. The moulds are now slowly heated to melt out the wax from the cast. Next, the molten bell-metal alloy is prepared from zinc, tin and copper in a clay crucible. The precise moment for pouring the molten alloy into the mould is very critical and considerable skill and experience are needed to determine it. It can take several hours, using the crude facilities available, for the alloy to reach a molten state. Once the alloy is poured into the mould, it is allowed to cool, after which the clay mould is broken away to reveal the newly-formed bell inside. After careful cleaning, grinding and polishing, the clappers and wind leaves are added, and the finished article is ready to be fixed at the rafter ends. Bell-making was undertaken by several Tamrakar families in Patan and it was a common sight to see clutches of bells hanging in windows in different stages of preparation.

Kathmandu

Kathmandu City is the hub of the Kathmandu Valley wheel, with the Durbar Square and the Royal Palace at its centre. From the airport—located between the three major cities of Kathmandu, Bhaktapur and Patan—you will enter Kathmandu from the southeast and most probably head towards your accommodation in the newer part of the city, either on Durbar Marg, in Maharajgunj, or in Kalimati.

Kathmandu has expanded rapidly over the last decade, with new buildings of all shapes, sizes and uses strung along the old trade routes. The once common vista of paddy fields within the city confines has been replaced with unsightly concrete jungles but occasionally you will find a small oasis—an old palace compound or a family plot hidden between the buildings.

To reach old Kathmandu you will need to take a taxi or rickshaw and penetrate the old and winding alleys or skirt the edge of the old city along Judha Sadak (New Road) to the Kathmandu Durbar Square and the Hanuman Dhoka where your journey into the past will begin.

Experience first the people, the buildings and the ambience in the old city; get your bearings in this unfamiliar culture before delving deeply into the history and architecture; a little understanding of the vibrant culture of Nepal will help you to comprehend the experiences you have before you.

Hanuman Dhoka Durbar

The Hanuman Dhoka in Kathmandu is the most fascinating of the three durbar squares of the Kathmandu Valley. The other two are in Patan and Bhaktapur (see pages 118–24, and 102–110). The tour through the Kathmandu Durbar Square will take you first through the accessible parts of the palace and afterwards to some of the associated buildings to be found around the palace complex.

There is no building in the present Hanuman Dhoka complex that dates back to before the Malla period. However, there is every indication that the present site of the durbar could have been used in the Lichhavi period. As it stands today, this old royal palace spans many centuries and different building styles and uses. The complex is made up of at least ten different courtyards or *chowks*. The original Malla durbar covered only two of them—the existing Mohan Chowk and one other that has subsequently disappeared. Guarding the entrance to the palace is **Hanuman** (15), the monkey god, after whom the palace is named. He was believed to be a great patron of the Mallas as they claimed descent from Ram Chandra, to whom Hanuman's devotion was legendary. The symbol of Hanuman was therefore used extensively by the Mallas and his image was generally placed at the entrance to their palaces as protection and to bring victory in war. The stone image of Hanuman at the entrance of the Durbar was erected by Pratap Malla in 1672. It is difficult to recognize the features of the monkey as it is covered in an ever-thickening layer of red *tikka*, an offering that devotees place on its forehead. Periodically, a new red cape is draped over its shoulders and the specially decorated umbrella is changed yearly.

To the right of Hanuman, the **Golden Door** (15) of the main entrance to the palace is flanked by a pair of stone lions, ridden by Shiva on the left and Shakti on the right. They too probably date from Malla times. The door itself is of a later period. An inscription dates its construction to 1810. The funds for this piece of extravagance were provided by gathering hundreds of outdated copperplate inscriptions which were then sold to provide the gold for its gilding. Above the Golden Door are three interesting images. The central figures are said to be Krishna, Biswarupa and Arjuna in a scene from the *Mahabharata* (see pages 108–9). To the left of this group, Krishna is seen with his two favourite *gopinis*, Rukmini and Satyabhama. The third group is of a king and queen. The king's features represent those of Pratap Malla and the three groups were possibly set up by him.

Passing through the Golden Door you enter the **Nasal Chowk** (23), the largest of the courtyards in the palace. Its existing dimensions date from the beginning of the Shah Dynasty, as it was at this time that the courtyard became the meeting place for the nobles of all Nepal, as opposed to those of the kingdom of Kantipur alone. The name of the courtyard is derived from the deity Nasaleswar, the dancing Shiva, whose shrine is the rather insignificant white structure opposite the entrance on the eastern side. During the Malla period, Nasal Chowk served as a royal theatre, and dances and drama were rehearsed and performed there. It also became the gathering place for meetings between the king and his people. During the Shah Dynasty, the courtyard was extended to accommodate guests for the coronation rites. Previously, the Mallas had always conducted these ceremonies in the much smaller Mul Chowk. As you move into the courtyard, you will be struck by the overpowering scale and variety of buildings surrounding you. Just to the left of the entrance you will see a very imposing **image of Narasingha** (24) , the half-man half-lion, one of the ten incarnations of Vishnu. This sculpture of black marble, decorated with silver and gold, was probably imported from India. It was installed by Pratap Malla in 1673 to appease Narasingha, whom he thought he had offended when he danced in public dressed as a deity. Beyond the image, and opening into the courtyard, is the **Sisa Baitak**, the audience chamber of the Malla kings. It is a long, spacious verandah-like room open to the south and it still contains the simple throne of the Mallas.

In a portico under the finely carved balcony window of the Vilas Mandir is a very fine gilded-bronze **image of Maha Vishnu** which was rescued from the debris after the 1934 earthquake. It is only recently that the upper heads of the deity have been replaced by craftsmen from Patan and the statue dedicated again following a special ceremony.

In the centre of the courtyard is a large, low platform. Although traditions connected with this platform go back hundreds of years, its present shape dates from 1826, when much of the latest part of the palace was constructed and the courtyard was partly stone-paved. Each year, during Indrajatra, the image of Indra is brought from the Degutaleju Temple (see page 76) and placed on the platform, a tradition that probably survives from the time of the Mallas. Recently, the platform was the focal point of King Birendra's coronation; it was here that the throne was placed, as it has been for several reigns, and the crowned king received the homage of his subjects.

Looking back and above the Gaddi Baitak, you will notice two small towers rising out of the building. At the northwest corner is the **Agam Chen** which houses the traditional family shrine of the Malla kings. Entrance to the shrine has always been restricted; to this day its sanctity remains inviolate even though the Malla kings have long ceased to rule. Directly across the rooftop from the Agam Chen, on the northeast corner, is a five-tiered tower of the **Panch Mukhi Hanuman**, the five-faced monkey. Although there is no inscription, the temple apparently dates from the year 1655. Worship of Hanuman is offered daily according to secret rites and only the resident priest may enter the temple.

To the north of Nasal Chowk lies **Mohan Chowk** (10), the residence of the Malla kings. It was built by Pratap Malla in 1649 and later 'modernized' and repaired during the reign of King Rajendra Bikram Shah in 1822. At present, for religious and security reasons, foreigners are not permitted to enter this courtyard. One of its central features is a fine, gilded water-spout, set in a beautifully carved sunken bathing area. It was here that the king performed his ritual bathing ceremonies, after which he ascended the large stone throne to complete his morning devotions. Close at hand is a globe of the world, unrecognizable today, but which Pratap Malla studied in an attempt to understand the world around him.

Mohan Chowk is built in the *chowkath* form, a square quadrangle with towers at each corner. The building itself is three storeys high, with a magnificent balconied window on the eastern wall. In niches around the walls are several scenes of the life of Krishna carved in wood. It is hoped that King Birendra will soon permit foreigners to enter these courtyards.

Another courtyard that played an important part in the daily life of the Malla kings was the **Mul Chowk** (17), or main courtyard, situated behind the low roofs on the eastern side of Nasal Chowk. Mul Chowk was the scene of almost all the truly important functions of the Malla period. Religious rites of all descriptions, royal weddings, the investiture of crown princes and ministers, as well as the coronation of kings took place in this small court-yard. This *chowk* represents one of the earliest examples of Nepal's standing buildings. Built by Mahendra Malla in 1564, at the same time as he was

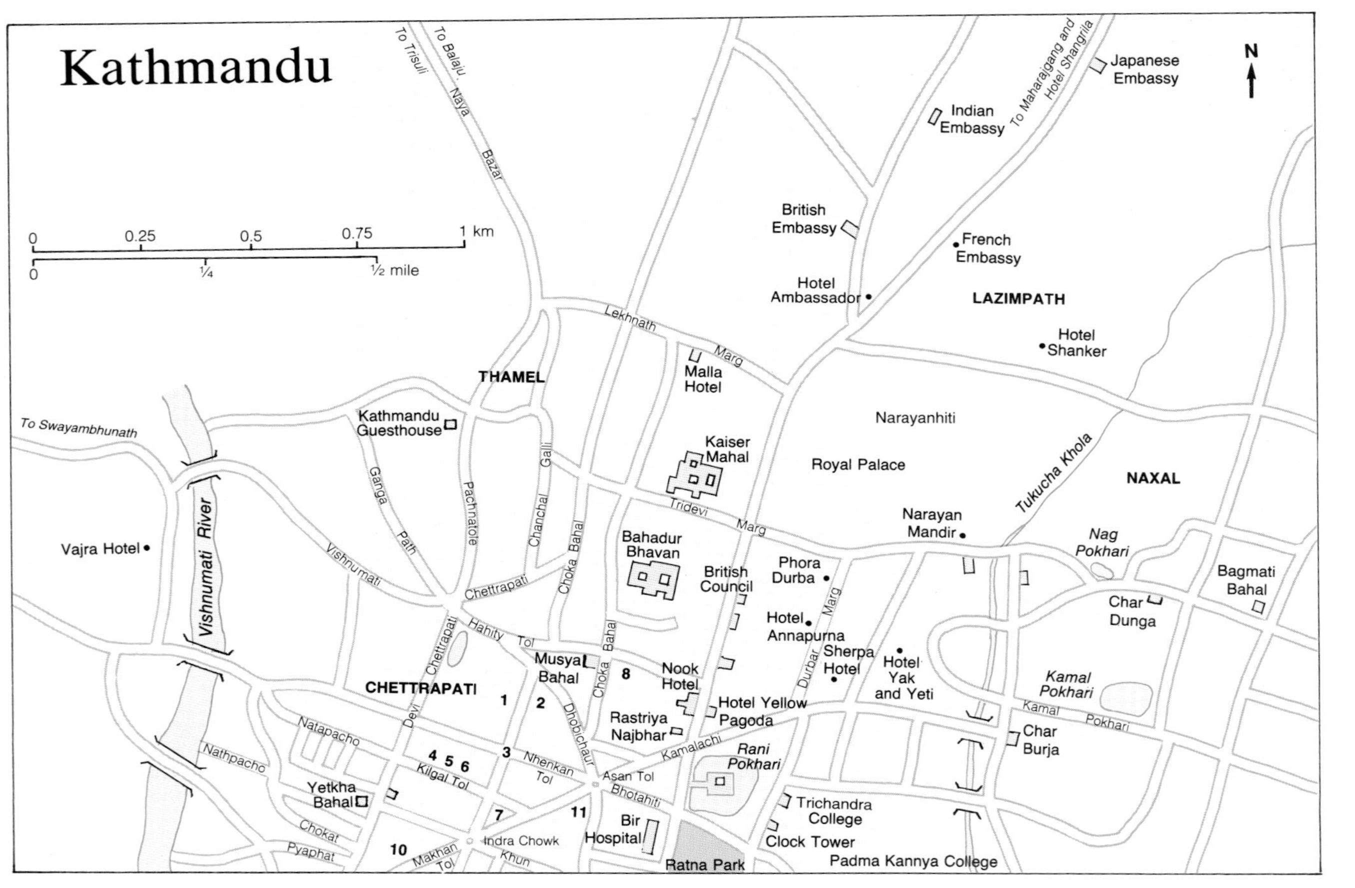
Kathmandu
N
0
0.25
0.5
0.75
1 km
0
¼
½ mile
To Trisuli
To Balaju
Naya Bazar
To Maharajgang and Hotel Shangrila
Japanese Embassy
Indian Embassy
British Embassy
French Embassy
Hotel Ambassador
LAZIMPATH
Hotel Shanker
Lekhnath Marg
Malla Hotel
THAMEL
Narayanhiti
Royal Palace
To Swayambhunath
Kathmandu Guesthouse
Kaiser Mahal
Tukucha Khola
NAXAL
Tridevi Marg
Narayan Mandir
Nag Pokhari
Vajra Hotel
Vishnumati River
Ganga Path
Pachnatole
Chanchal Galli
Choka Bahal
Vishnumati
Bahadur Bhavan
British Council
Phora Durba
Bagmati Bahal
Char Dunga
Chettrapati
Hahity Tol
Musya Bahal
Hotel Annapurna
Durbar Marg
Sherpa Hotel
Hotel Yak and Yeti
Kamal Pokhari
Nook Hotel
8
CHETTRAPATI
1
2
Hotel Yellow Pagoda
Rastriya Najbhar
Kamal Pokhari
Char Burja
Natapacho
Devi Chettrapati
3
Nhenkan Tol
Dhobichaur
Kamalachi
Rani Pokhari
Nathpacho
4 5 6
Kilgal Tol
Asan Tol
Bhotahiti
Yetkha Bahal
7
11
Trichandra College
Chokat
Pyaphat
10
Makhan Tol
Indra Chowk
Khun
Bir Hospital
Ratna Park
Clock Tower
Padma Kannya College

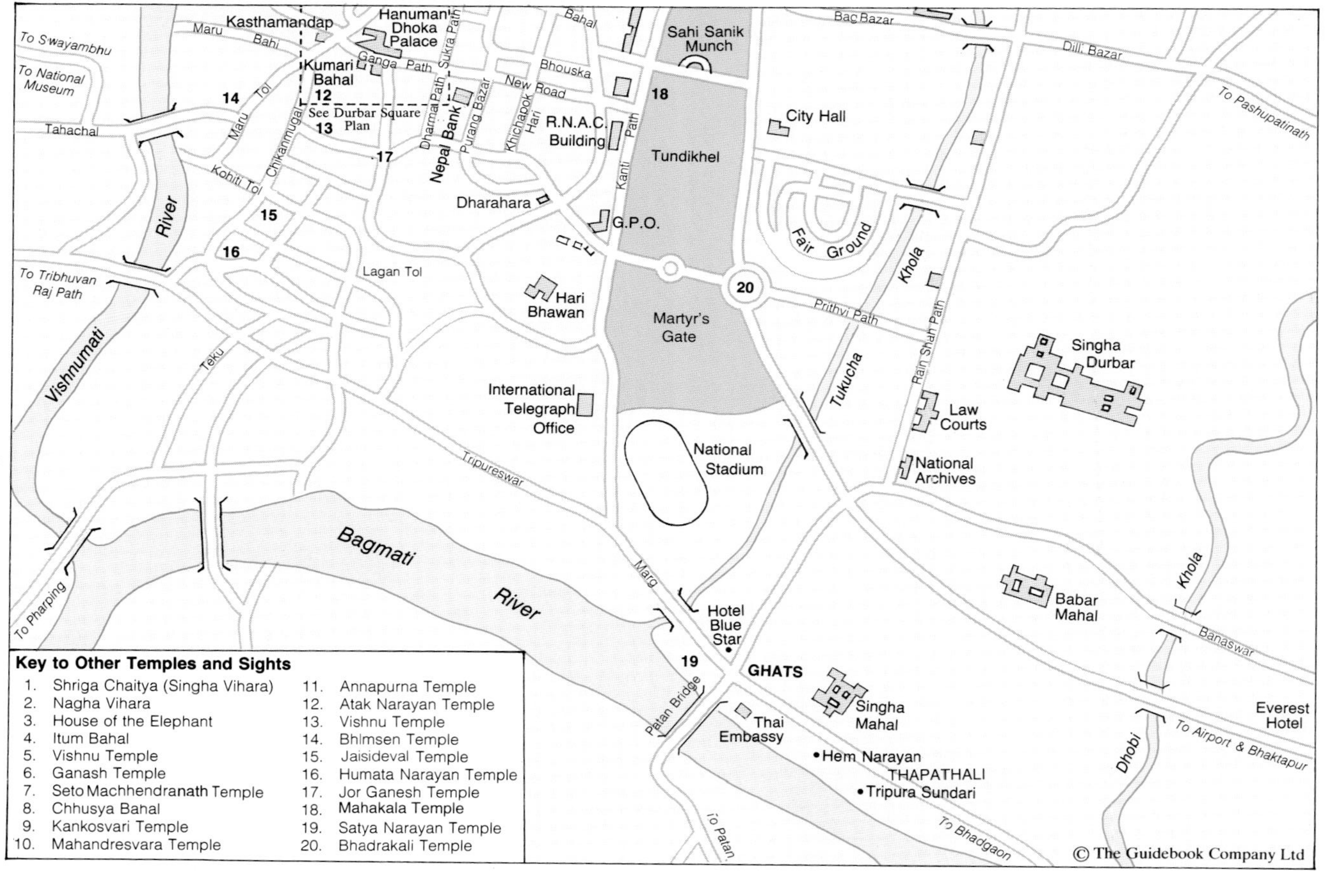
Kasthamandap
Hanuman Dhoka Palace
Maru Bahi
To Swayambhu
To National Museum
Kumari Bahal
12
13
14
Maru Tol
See Durbar Square Plan
Ganga Path
Sukra Path
Dharma Path
Nepal Bank
Purang Bazar
Khichapok
Hari
New Road
Bhouska
Bahal
R.N.A.C. Building
Kanti Path
Sahi Sanik Munch
18
Tundikhel
City Hall
Bag Bazar
Dilli Bazar
To Pashupatinath
Tahachal
Chikanmugal
17
Kohiti Tol
15
16
Dharahara
G.P.O.
River
To Tribhuvan Raj Path
Lagan Tol
Hari Bhawan
Fair Ground
Khola
20
Martyr's Gate
Prithvi Path
Rain Shah Path
Singha Durbar
Vishnumati
Teku
International Telegraph Office
Tukucha
Law Courts
National Stadium
National Archives
Tripureswar
Bagmati
River
Marg
Hotel Blue Star
Khola
Babar Mahal
To Pharping
19
GHATS
Banaswar
Patan Bridge
Singha Mahal
Thai Embassy
Everest Hotel
Hem Narayan
THAPATHALI
Tripura Sundari
Dhobi
To Airport & Bhaktapur
To Patan
To Bhadgaon
© The Guidebook Company Ltd
Key to Other Temples and Sights
1. Shriga Chaitya (Singha Vihara)
2. Nagha Vihara
3. House of the Elephant
4. Itum Bahal
5. Vishnu Temple
6. Ganash Temple
7. Seto Machhendranath Temple
8. Chhusya Bahal
9. Kankosvari Temple
10. Mahandresvara Temple
11. Annapurna Temple
12. Atak Narayan Temple
13. Vishnu Temple
14. Bhlmsen Temple
15. Jaisideval Temple
16. Humata Narayan Temple
17. Jor Ganesh Temple
18. Mahakala Temple
19. Satya Narayan Temple
20. Bhadrakali Temple

building the Taleju Mandir close by, it was changed to its present form in 1709 by Bhaksar Malla.

Mul Chowk is shaped very much like a *vihara*, being a square courtyard surrounded by double-storeyed buildings. The southern wing contains a shrine housing the image of Taleju. In the middle of the courtyard is a low post set into the ground, to which the animals that are sacrificed during Dasain and Chaitra Dasain (see pages 169 and 174) are tied before they are decapitated with a single stroke of a *khukri*—the Gorkha sword. Mul Chowk is almost totally given over to the goddess Taleju. Her mark is everywhere. Most of the very beautifully carved roof struts depict scenes based on the stories of the *Chandi*, in which the *devi* is depicted in the act of destroying some demon. Below the level of the roof struts, these exploits are further described in inscriptions. All the balconied windows are exquisite, although much of their beauty is spoilt by the paintwork. The shrine in which the Taleju *devi* is placed during the major festival of Dasain is richly decorated with gilded doors, windows and tympanum. Flanking the doors are two life-size images of Ganga and Jamuna. A gilded pinnacle marks the roof of the shrine, and in front of this are five more gilded pinnacles which mark the sanctuary itself. Again, access to this *chowk* is restricted to members of the palace, save for one day during Dasain, when Hindus alone are permitted to pay homage to Taleju. It is, however, possible to see something of the courtyard from the terrace above the Vilas Mandir.

At the southeast corner of Nasal Chowk there is an exit leading into **Lohăn Chowk**, a stone-paved courtyard surrounded by a three-storeyed building, the **Vilas Mandir** (26), or 'Building of Luxury'. This section of the palace was the subject of a major conservation project undertaken by the Nepal Government in collaboration with the UNDP and UNESCO (see the Hanuman Dhoka Conservation Project, pages 69–73). At each corner of this structure stand towers, including the tall Basantapur Tower which overlooks the rest of the palace buildings. This used to be the early residence of the Shah kings. They moved from the quarters formerly occupied by the Malla kings into this section of the durbar during Prithvi Narayan Shah's reign. The structure was greatly enlarged and, to commemorate his conquest of the Valley and the unification of Nepal, Prithvi Narayan Shah built or, more likely, extended the present Basantapur Tower to its present height. According to the inscription over its main entrance, the tower in its present form was completed on 21 March 1770 and named *Basant*, meaning Spring, as this season was being heralded in by the festival of Basant Panchami (see page 167).

The architectural history of this whole complex of buildings is a little confused. The recent repair works have indicated that it has been added to and extended over several different periods, and research on a comparative basis has established that the lower half of the Basantapur Tower is adorned with carvings and inscriptions of a period before 1630. A second period of building can quite clearly be established: the enlarging of the palace took place under Prithvi Narayan Shah's guidance after he had established himself in this durbar. A third building period appears to have taken place under the supervision of Prithvi Narayan's son, Pratap Singh Shah, on his father's death. It was at this time that the upper floor of the Vilas Mandir and the three remaining towers were built. The towers were named after the towns that donated and built them in recognition of the unification of the Valley and Nepal. There is also a theory that they replaced some earlier towers, as the names of the present towers do not tally with those recorded in the chronicles.

This group of buildings was occupied by the Shah Dynasty for only a hundred years, until the mid-19th century. The buildings have since served more as a backdrop for ceremonial occasions. When UNESCO undertook the Hanuman Dhoka Conservation Project in 1972, the buildings were being used as government offices and storage space for government archives.

A Tour through the Hanuman Dhoka Conservation Project

On the next few pages are recorded many of the Hanuman Dhoka Project team's experiences during the four and a half years that the programme was operational. It was here that the renaissance of the traditional crafts and craftsmen took place during the building's repair and so, during your tour around, you will not only be able to witness some of Nepal's most beautiful carvings, but also be able to learn and appreciate something of the traditional crafts of Nepal.

For purposes of orientation, we shall take the nine-storeyed Basantapur Tower as being in the southwest corner, facing north across Nasal Chowk. At the northwest corner is the Kirtipur Tower, often referred to as the Bangla Tower. It has a domed copper roof of distinct Bengali influence. Opposite, at the northeastern corner, is the Bhaktapur Tower, a building of traditional construction but octagonal-plan form. The remaining tower dominating the Juddha Sadak, or New Road, is the Lalitpur Tower, a solid square structure that had a severe lean as a result of the 1934 earthquake. It was only recently, during the conservation programme, that this dramatic failing was rectified.

As a starting point, let us take the Basantapur Tower, the imposing elevation overlooking Nasal Chowk. It is hard now to believe that every square centimetre of it was once covered in paint. Up to eight layers were removed from some of the lower, carved timbers where all the details in the carvings of the windows and cornices had been obliterated. The brickwork, with its unique glazing, was hidden under layers of red distemper, the intention being no doubt to unify the facade as the upper level had been

constructed in an unglazed brick of inferior quality. The magnificent double-storeyed window consists of well over 500 interlocking pieces. The detail in it is unbelievable, even down to the individual horses and birds, the miniature rampant lions and the hundreds of specially turned pieces that form the lower fringe. The door leading into the Lohan Chowk is one of the largest of its kind. Again, there is amazing detail: hundreds of skulls forming a border to the doorframe, entwining snakes, and a fine carving of Ganesh over the lintel.

It is well worth considering the exquisite carvings on the lower half of the Basantapur Tower. These undoubtedly represent some of the finest examples of woodcarving to be found in Nepal. The erotic carvings at the base of the struts and the inscriptions provided the information necessary to date these works of art, and possibly to give sufficient evidence to date the building itself. It is worth studying the details of the windows—the birds being chased by dogs, and vice versa, up the jambs of the lower windows—and to pick out the first example of a soldier armed with a gun in the sill of the lower right-hand window, or just to gaze upon the serene faces of the deity and his consort in the supporting roof struts.

The Vilas Mandir

Climbing the stairs up the Basantapur Tower, you will reach the terrace over the Vilas Mandir, or the Lohan Chowk as it was originally known, and from here it is possible to study the three towers.

The **Kirtipur Tower** has a Bengali-style roof covered with copper sheets that were originally gilded. In all aspects this structure is unique in Nepal and presented many difficulties when it came to rectifying its faults. The tower was in a state of near collapse. The copper sheeting had been nailed direct to the boarding and rainwater had penetrated the nail holes. On either side of the ridge of the roof, where the curve is flatter, water had seeped in between the overlapping joints and caused the timbers to decay, the nails to loosen and the copper sheets to become unfixed. The general condition of the timbers led to a further weakening of the structure and, as a result of several earth tremors, the timber joints had failed completely.

Eighty percent of the timbers were not reusable. To compound the problem, there was not a single straight member in the whole roof structure. The tower, therefore, had to be completely dismantled and careful records and drawings made so that the original roof design could be reassembled correctly. Every piece of carving was referenced before being handed over to one of the carving sections and each structural member was carefully dismantled, similarly recorded and passed to the carpenters.

Perhaps the most arduous task was the preparation of the curved rafters, all of which had to be replaced. It was particularly difficult to determine the shape of the original complete rafters as most of these were damaged. The pit sawyers were persuaded to cut the timbers on a curve, something they had never done before. At the same time as the carpenters were working on the repair and replacement of the structure, the carvers were repairing and replacing the damaged sections of carvings. The preparatory work took nearly nine months and about four additional months were required for the careful fitting together of all the pieces of this major jigsaw. As a protection against further decay from fungal or beetle attack, each timber was dipped in a chemical bath.

The copper roof covering posed further difficulties. As the original roof covering had outlived its use, the old copper sheeting was carefully removed and used as templates for the new copper sheets so that they matched the original in outward appearance and size. The fixing was incorporated into the welded joints so as not to pierce the waterproof copper membrane.

This repair work was carried out so as to reproduce faithfully the original pieces, even down to the metal fixings that were hand forged in the original manner. However, because of the great expense, the roof was not gilded.

The mighty **Basantapur Tower** (21), rising about 30.5 metres (100 feet) from the ground, posed a totally different set of problems. Its sheer size was the most daunting problem, especially using bamboo to scaffold it. At first the idea of bamboo, as opposed to solid tubular steel, caused considerable concern. The work involved cutting and transporting the bamboos from the forests, erecting the many pieces and tying them together with thousands of metres (yards) of string. Despite all these difficulties and after initially training the scaffolders to tie safety knots for the lashings and to observe basic principles of safety, a team of 20 to 30 men set to work on the task. The scaffolding became the centre of speculation in Kathmandu for some time as there was little visible progress on its erection for several months. The topmost roof required major structural repair since it was damaged during the 1934 earthquake. A new structural base to the roof was inserted, replacing the old, decayed and damaged timbers. The pinnacle and its base measured 4.6 metres (15 feet) long by 1.5 metres (five feet) wide and stood three metres (ten feet) above the roof. This had to be dismantled and lowered to the ground by means of a home-made block and tackle. It was then repaired and the traditional interlocking joints were rationalized. Previously, they had caused inherent weaknesses in the structure. All the timbers were also treated against further beetle and fungal attack.

The repair programme on the square **Lalitpur Tower** (20) posed some of the most interesting technical problems so far encountered. Unlike the two towers in the first stage, where the problems of repair and renovation were not clearly visible, the failings of the Lalitpur Tower were a major attraction visible from along New Road (Juddha Sadak). Its notorious lean of over 15 degrees from vertical was caused by the 1934 earthquake. It had not collapsed because, shortly after it was damaged, some German engineers are said to have propped the building in its leaning condition to protect it from total collapse. It survived thus for just over 40 years.

Careful initial examination of the structure showed the actual breaking-point of the lean to be where the solid brick walling ended and the flexible timber framework took over. This framework, consisting of an unbraced post-and-lintel structure supporting a very heavy roof, was also supporting externally complete façades of carved windows. The reason for failure was the lack of any diagonal bracing in the structure. Fortunately, because of the structure's flexibility, the failure took place at the joints. Apart from a few warped or twisted members, almost all the structural and decoratively carved timbers were reusable. The roof, being a well-designed and well-built hipped structure, but of very heavy construction, only slid in a horizontal direction and the eaves remained parallel to the floor after the earthquake. We are told the tiles stayed undisturbed on the roof.

Because of the structure's flexibility and the excellent condition of the roof, it was hoped, originally, to lighten the roof structure by taking off some of the easily removable carved work and physically jacking the building back into an upright position as a demonstration of the many possibilities in the field of building-repair. It was soon discovered during preliminary investigations that much of the structure supporting even the brickwork to the tower was in a very dangerous state. Also, much of the carved woodwork on the south elevation was badly weathered due to its excessive exposure to the elements. It was then necessary to carefully dismantle the building following the technique so well tested and proven in the first stage.

Due to considerable movement caused by the earthquake, the structure beneath the tower had opened up enough to allow rainwater to percolate the timber supports, causing extensive structural failure almost to the point of collapse. With the judicious insertion of concrete beams and bonders in the brickwork to replace the vulnerable timber structure, and having rebuilt the badly damaged north wall, a firm base for the upper section of the tower was formed. Next, the inner structure was erected, both level and plumb, and to strengthen the framework and prevent the lateral weaknesses, diagonal bracing, using specially tailored angle irons, was inserted between the vertical posts and fixed horizontal members to form a kind of lattice girder around the upper part of the structure.

The roof was replaced using over 90 percent of the original structural members which had been duly referenced, only to find that once they were cleaned a previous numbering system in Newari had been used!

The standard repair work, cleaning and conservation techniques, which were tested and proved to be both a successful and a viable proposition in the first stage, were used again to complete the work on this tower. The final result is a fine tribute to the craftsmen who worked on its renovation.

Unlike the other three towers which were in a very poor condition, the octagonal **Bhaktapur Tower** (19) had withstood most of the devastation that had affected the others. In fact, the work needed to be carried out was merely basic maintenance. It was originally intended to clean the roof members and the carvings *in situ*, but as the team of carpenters had by now perfected the technique of dismantling and reassembling complicated structures and the cleaning of the long roof members was very much easier when dismantled, the rafters and internal supports were taken down. This gave easier access to the carved windows which could now be cleaned *in situ*. Owing to the nature of the structural plan of the tower—a square with the corners cut off to form an octagon at the point where the timber framework supersedes the brick-work—it was able to withstand the earthquake without major failure. The roof, its covering and the carved windows remained intact, with only very local disturbance. The work then carried out was of a general nature, consisting of re-roofing to incorporate the new techniques evolved in the first stage and the cleaning and treatment of the woodwork of both the carved windows and the roof structure. The complex roof pattern was a real challenge to the traditional roof tilers and no doubt their skills have gone a long way to enhance this very decorative and unusual tower.

A Tour through the Durbar Square

Perhaps the best place to survey the celebrated **Taleju Mandir** (9) is from atop the towers of Vilas Mandir. This very impressive structure, built in 1564 by Mahendra Malla, is the most splendid, and famous, of the three Taleju

Mandirs built by the Malla kings in the Valley. The worship of Taleju Devi came to Kathmandu Valley with refugees from Terai and the god became the tutelary deity of the Mallas at the time of Jayastithi Malla's assumption of power. When the Valley was divided into several kingdoms after 1428, the various branches of the Malla family built their own shrines to Taleju near their palaces. This Taleju Mandir is in the Trisul Chowk and can be reached by the Singh Dhoka. The temple is over 37 metres (122 feet) high, rests on a 12-stage plinth, and has three gilded roofs. It used to be the highest structure in Kathmandu; tradition had it that it was inauspicious to build higher. Sadly, this simple rule is no longer adhered to, as modern high-rise buildings mar the roofscapes.

The temple is of impressive size and everything about it—the doors, windows and supporting roof struts—are of similar proportions. The south-facing door and the *torana* are gilded and the windows elsewhere are all heavily carved. The imagery throughout is indicative of the Shakta cult. Everything about the temple seems to emphasize its ritual remoteness. The roofs of all three stages are of gilded copper and edged with rows of wind-bells. The corners of the two lower roofs are decorated with embossed banners, while the upper roof has specially designed pots hanging from each corner and is capped with a very beautiful pinnacle. Beautifully proportioned and in a wonderful setting, it is undoubtedly one of the finest buildings in the traditional style and perhaps the most dramatic and yet pleasing structure in the Valley.

The Durbar Square

Leaving the marvels of art and architecture behind, we shall now take a closer look around the Durbar Square. The large temple opposite the Hanuman gate is the **Jagannath** (25), which was originally built by Mahendra Malla in 1563. In the inner recess of the shrine is an important **image of the Chaturmurti Vishnu** with an inscription bearing this date. The inscription, in Sanskrit, is the earliest yet found in the Hanuman Dhoka. The Jagannath rests on a three-tiered platform and has a two-tiered roof supported by some very elaborately carved roof struts famed for their erotic carvings. Like those of the Hanuman Dhoka, these show a Tantric influence. Unusually, each of the four elevations contains groups of three doors that are of excellent quality. The central door in each case carries the signs of Mahadev, three eyes and a trident, and on each of the other doors are the symbols of the Shakta cult to represent the goddess: three indentations above a decorative pot. The temple has an inner sanctuary into which only the priests may go. Above the roofs of the palace buildings, on the left-hand side of the golden door, is the magnificent **Degutaleju Temple** (34) which appears to grow out of the lower structure. It was built by Shiva Singh Malla in the late 16th cen-

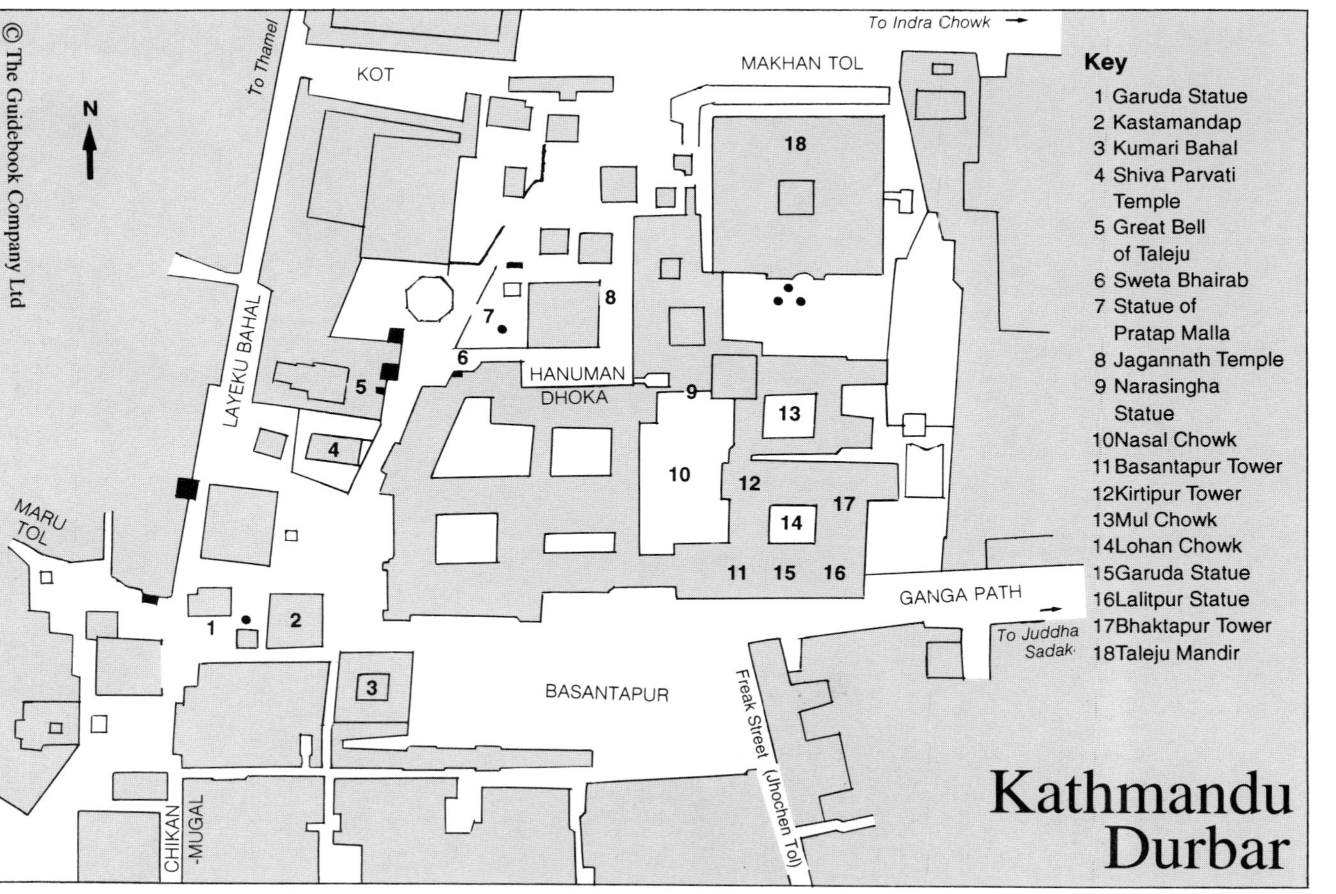
Kathmandu Durbar
Key
1 Garuda Statue
2 Kastamandap
3 Kumari Bahal
4 Shiva Parvati Temple
5 Great Bell of Taleju
6 Sweta Bhairab
7 Statue of Pratap Malla
8 Jagannath Temple
9 Narasingha Statue
10 Nasal Chowk
11 Basantapur Tower
12 Kirtipur Tower
13 Mul Chowk
14 Lohan Chowk
15 Garuda Statue
16 Lalitpur Statue
17 Bhaktapur Tower
18 Taleju Mandir
To Indra Chowk
MAKHAN TOL
KOT
To Thamel
N
LAYEKU BAHAL
HANUMAN DHOKA
MARU TOL
BASANTAPUR
GANGA PATH
To Juddha Sadak
Freak Street (Jhochen Tol)
CHIKAN-MUGAL
© The Guidebook Company Ltd

tury and was later added to by Shah kings. The temple is about 28 metres (93 feet) high, slightly shorter than the Taleju Mandir, and belongs to a different manifestation of the Shakta cult. Again, this is a special royal temple and it can only be reached through the living quarters of the palace terrace. The temple rises above this terrace with a three-tiered roof, richly ornamented. The north-facing door is panelled in silver, the gift of King Girnbana Yuddha Bikram Shah in 1815. The top roof is capped with a very fine pinnacle.

Set high on a pillar opposite the Degutaleju Temple is a **statue of Pratap Malla** (27), the founder of much of the art and architecture that surrounds him. He is accompanied by his four sons and two of his wives. This is an exquisite piece of metalwork and the first of its kind depicting the king in an attitude of praise before his favourite temple.

Almost beneath the Degutaleju is the large golden **mask of Sweta Bhairab** (13), fierce in appearance and standing at least four metres (12 feet) high. It is normally screened from public view, but is exposed during Indrajatra in September, when the local beer pours from its mouth to be gulped down by an excited crowd. The image was erected by Rana Bahadur Shah in 1796 to drive off evil spirits and ghosts.

Mention should be made of the **Great Drums** (29) across the road, which were installed at the beginning of the 19th century and are beaten during the worship of the Degutaleju. About the same time, the great bell was erected by King Rana Bahadur Shah to drive off evil spirits.

Adjacent to the great drums there is an unusual octagonal temple, **the Krishna Temple** (28), which was built by Pratap Malla in 1637. When Siddhi Narasingha was dedicating the famous Krishna Temple of Patan (see page 110), Pratap Malla, who was only a prince, attacked the city. His efforts were largely futile but he received a great deal of criticism and, in order to regain some of his lost prestige, he built this temple in memory of his two queens. Again, a Sanskrit inscription tells us that the features on the images in the shrine resemble those of Pratap and his queens. The construction of the temple is slightly more complicated owing to its shape, but the three-tiered roof structure is supported by some well-carved roof struts.

Here we must leave the section of Durbar Square adjacent to the Hanuman Dhoka and move into the main part of the square where there is a further profusion of temples. As you walk up the short street that joins the two open spaces, the buildings on the left are, in fact, the west wing of one of the original Malla courtyards. It is known as **Masan Chowk** (12), which translated literally means 'cremation courtyard'. An interesting theory suggests that this building-group actually represents today the northwesternmost corner of old Kathmandu, as it was common for such a courtyard to be placed on the outer extremities of the palace complex and orientated in such a way. This building, which had formerly been used as a shopping arcade and condemned as structurally unsound, has been the subject of an interesting piece of building conservation. The original structure had been badly damaged by the 1934 earthquake and you can see today the effect of this damage in the leaning and bulging walls. The members of the Hanuman Dhoka Conservation Project Office, who were called in to advise on the structure, felt that this building, as it stood with its leans and bulges, was such an important and historical feature in the streetscape that it should be consolidated in its existing state. This was cleverly done by consolidating the structure with reinforced concrete columns and beams inserted in the thickness of the walls and floors. The building was carefully freed of its stucco finish to reveal the beautiful glazed brickwork. The special window at the corner, where the king is said to have sat watching his subjects, is an unusual and particularly fine example of traditional craftsmanship. Not only does it demonstrate fine woodcarving but also some beautiful gilded metalwork and, if you look closely, you will also see carvings in ivory and bone. The building now stands as an important focal point in the Durbar Square and maintains its character.

As you enter the second square on the right, an unusual **temple to Shiva and Parvati** (32) stands on what was probably a dance platform long before the temple was built in the late 18th century. This rectangular temple is unusual in form as, although it conforms in principle to the typical building style, its detail and construction are very different. It is likely that it was made up of various bits of an older building. The carvings are of an earlier period and the eastern windows of stone are unique. Overlooking the platform in the upper window of the temple are the images of Shiva and Parvati, his consort, who have always captured the imagination of the local people because of their poses and expressions which are so life-like.

The most imposing temple in the square is the dominating **Maju Deval** (36). Set in the centre of the square, it was built in 1690 by Riddhi Laxmi and is dedicated to Shiva. It is worth climbing the base of the temple for an overall view of the Durbar Square.

The next largest temple in the courtyard is the **Trailokya Mohan Temple** (37), which was built by Parthibendra Malla in 1680. It is often referred to as the Das Avatar Dekaune Mandir, as it is here, during the festival of Indrajatra (see page 174), that dances depicting the ten incarnations of Vishnu are performed. The temple is dedicated to Vishnu, and his vehicle Garuda can be found on the western side carved out of stone (41). This is one of the best examples of the Garuda to be found in the Valley. It was erected by Riddhi Laxmi nine years after the completion of the temple. Adjacent to this temple is a three-storeyed building with a traditional brick façade and some beautifully carved windows which have been recently renovated. It is in the form of a *bahal* (see page 49) and is the dwelling of the Kumari, the Living Goddess, who is a young virgin of the Shakya caste considered to be an incarnation of Taleju. The religious institution was founded by Jaya Prakash Malla in the mid-18th century and the construction of the *bahal* dates from the same period. The Kumari plays an important role during most of the Taleju festivals, but most spectacular is when she rides around the city in a chariot during the festival of Indrajatra. The worship of Kumari has strong Newari Buddhist influence, although many Hindus, including the royal family, pay their respects to her at the major festivals.

The **Kumari Bahal** (or Ghar as it is often called) has important socio-religious significance. It is built in the style of a Buddhist *bahal* and has a shrine to Buddha in the courtyard. The inner façades, like the main one, contain beautiful carved windows, doors and roof struts. The inner balcony windows are especially fine and it is here that the Kumari appears from time to time in the company of her guardians to see and be seen by her admirers.

Continuing west, towards the diagonal route from Maru Tol where the square narrows, there is a small building (45) that has more the appearance of a resthouse than a temple, although it is dedicated to Narayan. It is a very important building containing a wealth of interesting carvings. Its foundation date is unknown, but it appears to date from the 16th century. Today it has lost both its original function as well as its name. It was originally a *sattal* (see page 54) but later became a temple dedicated to Laxmi Narayan, when the addition on the north elevation was made. Today it serves as a money-changer's stall.

Before moving on to the majestic buildings of Maru Tol, a word about the small shrine—**Ashok Binayak** (39)—commonly called the **Maru Ganesh**, which is located in a corner adjacent to the Kasthamandap. Its size belies its importance, for this shrine is very popular in the Kathmandu Valley. It is one of four main shrines dedicated to Ganesh, and it is common practice to venerate Ganesh prior to carrying out other worship. The Kathmandu Ganesh is worshipped by the royal family, especially by the king, during the coronation ceremonies, and by both Hindus and Buddhists throughout the Valley. The entire surface of the shrine is gilded and, although there is no inscription, it is assumed to be fairly old. However, the present roof was added by King Surendra in 1847.

The third area of this extended Durbar Square, known as **Maru Tol**, is dominated by the **Kasthamandap** (42). This is not only the largest building of its style in the Valley, but also the oldest. The history of this dates back to the 14th century and many of the surviving timbers are thought to be of this period. Since the 16th century it has been known as the **Maru Sattal**. Legend has it that the timber used in the construction of the Kasthamandap came from a single tree which is said to have provided timber for the adjacent Singha Sattal as well.

The name 'Kasthamandap' translated literally means 'the wooden pavilion' and it is also the word from which the name Kathmandu is derived. The date of its construction is a little uncertain as the word used in the inscriptions for 'building' and 'renewing' is the same. Throughout its history there have been many changes and alterations to the Kasthamandap; nevertheless it is still remarkably like the descriptions of Nepali architecture given in the seventh-century Chinese travel books about Nepal.

The building consists of three large open halls set one above the other with a full balcony and low railings. Today there is a shrine dedicated to Goraknath but previously it was used by *sadhus*, who carried out the Tantric rites of the *Chakra Puja* here. The building has been recently restored to its present form and cleared of traders who had taken it over. Historically, it is perhaps the most important building in Kathmandu.

The other two important buildings in Maru Tol are the **Kabindrapur** (45), a four-storeyed building with three tiers of roofs, and the **Singha Sattal** (48). Kabindrapur, or Dhansa as it is sometimes referred to, is of rather special form. It was constructed by Pratap Malla in 1673 and dedicated to Narasingha as another form of appeasement for publicly miming him (see page 64). Pratap was a great patron of the arts, and he thought himself to be a literary person, well versed in song and dance; he adopted the name of Kabindra—master poet—hence the temple's name. This building was recently conserved and repaired by the Hanuman Dhoka Team to commemorate the state visit by Queen Elizabeth II of Great Britain.

Singha Sattal (or **Silyan**), so named after the leaping lions or griffons on the corners of the building, is a large house with shops below. The upper level is now used as a gathering place for the singing of *bhajans*. Inside there is an image of Garud Narayan, which was uncovered during excavations for a new house nearby in 1863. The bronze lions, however, were only put in place about 50 years ago.

Other Places to Discover in Kathmandu

The buildings or areas described below all are within half an hour's walk from the Durbar Square. Most of the buildings of interest are located on, or close to, the diagonal trade route between Bhimsenthan and Asan Tol, running through Maru Tol and the Durbar Square, to Indra Chowk, Asan and Bhotahiti. To the west of Maru Tol and the Durbar Square there are a few buildings of great interest that can be easily located.

At almost the southwestern extremity of the diagonal road is the **Bhimsen Temple**. As a protector and promoter of trades and crafts, Bhimsen became a popular god among the Newars in the 17th century. The temple was built in the mid-17th century and has no doubt undergone alterations and additions since then. It is of unusual form in that it is a two-storeyed temple with the main sanctuary on the upper floor and a row of shops below. The building is capped with two diminishing, gilded-metal roofs which are set over a lower, tiled roof. The shrine is not accessible to foreign visitors but it is interesting to watch the many devotees paying homage each morning. Formerly, the statue of Bhimsen was taken in procession every 12 years all the way to Lhasa in Tibet.

To the southeast of Bhimsenthan, at **Jaisideval**, is a largish temple of the late 17th century. Its location is said to have been the centre of Kathmandu during the Licchavi period as, on the eastern side of the temple, there is an early Licchavi inscription. Returning along the road, passing the Kasthamandap and crossing the Durbar Square, you reach **Makhan Tol** with its gold markets, and move into a road flanked by attractive arcaded buildings where cloth of all kinds and colours is sold. These buildings were modified in the late 19th century and, sadly, a large section of them has been torn down to be replaced by unsightly modern apartment blocks. At this point, it is worth looking back towards the Makhan Tol to see the splendidly located **Taleju Temple**—a building of magnificent proportions dominating a typical Kathmandu streetscape. This narrow and bustling street leads to a busy forecourt known as **Indra Chowk**, in front of the rather garish shrine of **Akash Bhairab**. This temple again follows the unusual form of an upper sanctuary, like that of Bhimsen, with shops below. The date of its construction is uncertain, but it does play an important part in many of the religious festivals, especially the festival of Indrajatra (see page 174), when a large mask of Bhairab, bedecked with flowers, is displayed in front of the temple. It is sometimes possible to enter the upper sanctuary to enjoy the *bhajan* at musical gatherings that take place in the evening.

Continuing along the main street, passing two temples on your left, you enter once again the narrow street of Asan, which is lined with traditional terraced dwellings with their shops and stores at ground level. The only warning you will get of the next important group of buildings will be a pair of pillars supporting griffons which protect the entrance to the **Seto Machhendra**. Entering through a narrow doorway, past a *bhajan* room on the right where music is played and sung nightly, you reach a courtyard of considerable proportions, in the centre of which is a very splendid temple with a two-tiered roof. This is a Buddhist shrine and one of the few monastic courtyards to have such a temple. The temple was built before the beginning of the 17th century but underwent renovations and alterations in the mid-17th and 19th centuries. It is highly ornamental, with gilt-copper roofs and a profusion of metal banners, prayer wheels and other decorations. The top roof is capped with an ornate pinnacle. The supporting roof struts at the lower level, clad in gilded metal, illustrate the diverse forms of the Avaloketeswar. The surrounding courtyard of paved stone is large and spacious, and has numerous small *chaityas* and stone pillars supporting Buddhist deities. There is also an interesting female figure of distinct European flavour supporting a lamp that must have come from one of the Rana palaces. The enshrined deity is Padmapani Avaloketeswar, the most compassionate divinity in the Valley, white in colour and commonly known as Janmadye or Machhendranath. He is the chief deity of the Machhendranath festival in Kathmandu which takes place in March (see page 169). Around the temple, the daily life mingling with the constant stream of worshippers is very typical of the Nepali way of life. Added to this, you may be fortunate enough to witness a family gathering or local festival taking place.

A small opening diagonally opposite the entrance leads to a pottery market, where pots of all shapes and sizes are brought from around the Valley to be sold. Moving through to the main road, you turn right, through an interesting collection of shops where cotton mattresses are made, to find yourself back on the diagonal road alongside a small temple with the strange name of **Lunchun Lun Bun Ajima**. The first thing you will notice is that the temple sanctuary is below the level of the road. Over the years the road has been repeatedly resurfaced. As a result, the level and indeed the water-table have risen as much as a foot (30 centimetres) above the original. This temple has beautiful proportions which the unpleasant white tiles added later to the façade cannot mar.

Continuing along the street towards Asan, you will find a very fine octagonal temple sandwiched between two residential buildings and projecting into the road. This is a **shrine to Krishna** and one of very few surviving polygonal temples. It has carvings of remarkable quality arcaded at ground-floor level, with fine pillars that support a series of exquisitely carved windows above. Directly adjacent to this temple, on its left, is an historically important residence of the early 19th century known as **Tilang Ghar**. It is famous as the first house in Kathmandu outside the palace to be permitted to use glass windows. Between the two floors on the façade is a stucco frieze depicting marching soldiers carrying guns. It is said to be a copy of a similar

frieze on one of King Prithvi Narayan Shah's fortifications at Nawakot in Trisuli.

Further along, the street broadens into the small square known as **Asan Tol**, where there are three small temples. The most interesting is the **Annapurna Temple**, hidden behind mounds of rice sold on its forecourt. This temple, which was possibly constructed in the early 19th century, belongs to a Buddhist Tantric sect and the object of worship in the sanctuary is not an image of a deity but a pot known as a *purnakalasha*. Here, symbols and mystic diagrams are used in worship rather than iconographic forms. Although it is primarily a Buddhist shrine, many non-Buddhists worship here. A particular form of worship known as *homa* is often performed here by a Bajacharya priest.

If you now take a turning to the left and follow the road between several small shops occupied by silversmiths, it will eventually open on to a square known as **Bangemuda**, where there is a group of fairly standard temples. By taking the left-hand turning you can return to Indra Chowk. At this corner you will notice a large baulk of timber with literally thousands of nails of all shapes and sizes driven into it. The placing of a nail in this timber is said to be a cure for toothache! It is also the quarter where all the dentists are to be found, no doubt on hand should the other cure fail.

From the New Road Gate to Narayan Hiti

Take the New Road Gate as a starting-point. If you face the large open parade ground, known as the Tundikhel, where all the military parades and massed gatherings take place, and turn left past the military and general hospitals, you will find, on the right-hand side, a temple on a raised level, known as **Mahakal**. Formerly, this location might have been a *bahal*, hence the small shrines on the opposite side of the road. This is a Buddhist temple housing one of the Buddhist tutelary divinities which usually stand guard at the entrance to Buddhist *viharas*. Mahakala is regarded as the protector of the land, and legend says that, while he was passing through the heavens, the famous Tantric preceptor, Manjubajra, bound him with *mantras* and enshrined him in this temple, which is one of the most worshipped in the Valley. People flock to it every morning on their way to work.

Following along the road you will reach **Rani Pokhari**, an extensive pond in the middle of which is a domed temple set on an island. This temple and pond, built in 1670 by Pratap Malla to console his wife on the death of their son, Chakrabartindra, are dedicated to Shiva. The present temple replaces an earlier one damaged during the earthquake in 1934, which was also a replacement of the original. Although access is difficult, it is possible to see some of the rather interesting statues and decorative elements that surround the pond, such as the magnificent stone elephants.

At the northwestern corner of the pond, continue along the road towards the new royal palace. Turning to the left beside the Nook Hotel, continue along this road until you come to a large building on your left that is guarded by a pair of ferocious stone lions set on either side of an entrance. This is the **Chhusya Bahal**, one of the oldest buildings of its kind still standing intact in the Valley. It closely follows the description given of a typical *bahal* but special note should be made of the very fine woodcarvings. The *bahal* was completed on 13 March 1649, and on the same day the stone statue of Harihara Lokeshvara was installed. The building, according to records, was not inaugurated by King Pratap Malla until 1667. The roof struts, said to date from the 15th century, are of particularly fine quality, and represent Pancharaksa and Pujadevi. Beneath these figures are carvings of the Nakshatras with inscribed illustrations. The beautifully carved *torana* over the entrance, dated 1673, illustrates the theme of Buddha's penance.

A short way further along the road is **Musya Bahal**, which is similar to Chhusya and constructed in 1663. The fading frescoes around the inner walls depict the Buddha and add to the monastic atmosphere. Again, the roof struts are beautifully carved and worthy of close inspection.

Either by retracing your steps or by wending a path through Thamel, you should make for the **Narayan Hiti**, adjacent to the new royal palace. Beyond the main entrance of the palace to the east, close to one of the entrances to the earlier palace, a flight of steps leads to the **Narayan Mandir**, which was built in 1793. This *shikhara*-style temple is set in a large and peaceful courtyard full of interesting small shrines. Close to the entrance of this temple, but on the other side of the road, are the water-spouts, the Narayan Hiti, which gave the palace its name. The tank has recently undergone major restoration. Inside you will find two of the flanking spouts, which resemble the heads of crocodiles with unusual grimaces on their faces. It is said that they witnessed the patricide of a certain King Dharmadeba who tricked his son into killing him in order to bring back the supply of water which had unaccountably dried up.

Returning to the Durbar Marg and close to the Hotel Annapurna, on the right-hand side, are the remains of a large Rana palace, the **Phora Durbar**, which was once a vast complex of palace buildings in a variety of European styles. It is said that this is only part of a facade that originally stretched over a kilometre (half a mile) and incorporated what remains of the **Lal Durbar** located in the Hotel Yak and Yeti complex. The palace boasted magnificent gardens and fountains as well as elaborate interiors panelled with mirrors and sparkling crystal chandeliers. This structure attempts to hold itself proudly in memory of its splendid past, but its future is far from assured.

Rana Palaces—A Bygone Era

The best known of the Rana palaces is undoubtedly the Singha Durbar which, until July 1974, stood intact as perhaps the last surviving complete example of this imported architectural pastiche. The palace is located on the eastern edge of Kathmandu and you will most likely pass it on the way to or from the airport. Sadly, much of the palace was razed to the ground by a devastating fire which destroyed all but the state rooms behind the main façade. This Baroque-style palace was the dream of Prime Minister 'Maharaja' Chandra Shamsher Jung Bahadur Rana who wanted to incorporate all his personal and official accommodation needs in one enormous edifice—almost a small city in itself. The palace was constructed in 1901 in just under one year with the guidance of the engineers Kumar and Kishor Singh and the labour of thousands of workers. In its former glory it consisted of over 1,700 rooms arranged around 17 open courtyards. Besides the magnificent state rooms, known as 'Belaiti Baitak'—the English Suite, many of which were decorated with interiors shipped straight from London and adorned with Belgian crystal—the palace boasted its own theatre with all the gimmickry required for a Vaudeville music hall. In its later years after the fall of the Ranas, the palace became the Government Secretariat. The original setting of this gigantic palace must have been spectacular, with its formal flower beds of exotic flowers and shrubs and beautifully manicured lawns.

The wing of the main façade and the formal entrance dominated by odd-shaped Corinthian columns supporting a meagre pediment are now all that remain of the original palaces. The gardens, with a central canal and fountains reflecting the classical symmetry of the main façade, are a small tribute to their former splendour. The state rooms are sometimes accessible—ask the guards at the gate—otherwise you can still conjure up the past grandeur of the Singha Durbar by strolling down the main drive admiring the statuary along the canal, glimpsing the old stables and the 'Hati Sar'—the Elephants Quarters, perhaps even hearing the drone of a bagpipe from the barracks close by.

After Chandra Shamsher made the Singha Durbar the official residence of the prime minister, he set about building several other important palaces to accommodate his sons. Among these were Sital Niwas—now the Royal Guest House half way up Maharajgung—and Kaiser Mahal. This palace still retains a remarkable library established by General Kaiser Shamsher but mostly houses the Ministry of Education and Culture. It is said that the Kaiser Mahal was modelled in miniature on the palace of Versailles in France but to find a comparison requires a lot of imagination.

If you are near the Yak and Yeti Hotel and happen to notice the large palace-like structure containing the main dining hall and the Crystal Room, you are looking at part of the old Lal Durbar, a palace that once had a main façade over a kilometre (half a mile) long with several variations on a neo-classical theme. Destroyed supposedly by fire in the 1950s, part of the same façade can be seen on the west side of the Durbar Marg which cuts right through the building.

Another accessible palace built by the Ranas is an extension of the traditional Hanuman Dhoka Palace, part of which now houses the museum of King Tribhuvan. The structure, which is enmeshed with the original Malla palace complex, overlooks the Nasal Chowk on the east side, extends on the west to the Kathmandu Durbar Square and to the south onto Basantapur. The latter part is known as the Gadhi Baitak, which was built at the beginning of this century and became the venue for all the major state functions. The building is said to have been a copy of the National Gallery in London, complete with its grand entrance steps, though these have now been removed.

The State Banks have taken over two other splendid palaces, thus assuring their maintenance. These are the impressive Singha Mahal in Thapathali and the Subarna Mahal in Baluwatar. Both buildings are multi-storeyed edifices with several internal courtyards and powerful façades, no doubt mimicking some vaguely recognizable European masterpiece.

In a commanding position in the southwestern corner of the Valley known as Kalimati are located the palaces known as Rabi Bhawan and the Kalimati Durbar. Kalimati Durbar is on a somewhat smaller scale than the other palaces described but has a collection of finely proportioned state rooms.

On the hill leading to Patan is the striking façade of Ananda Niketan, now occupied by the Engineering Institute. It is set back from the present road with an expanse of lawn in front of it.

Wandering through the outskirts of Patan or Kathmandu, you may happen upon the massive hulk of some forgotten and dilapidated palace inspired by some rococo counterpart in Italy—another fast-fading masterpiece which like its more unrestrained contemporaries, rightly deserves a corner in the history of the architecture of Nepal. These unique structures are disappearing quietly into oblivion, taking with them a colourful and exotic lifestyle of a bygone era.

Temples along the Bagmati River

For the next walk of discovery, it will be necessary to find some method of conveyance to the Patan Bridge, close to the Blue Star Hotel. This walk will take you along the shores of the holy Bagmati River: the area known as the **Ghats** or the place where Hindus cremate their dead. This area is used less extensively now and any cremations are conducted at the further end of the Ghats, at the confluence of the Vishnumati with the Bagmati.

The first temple you reach is the **Hem Narayan**, a building of obvious Mughal influence. It is a domed, stuccoed building, built on the instructions of Jung Bahadur Rana, the first Rana prime minister. There is a very fine gilded-bronze statue of him set on a stone pillar opposite the entrance to the shrine.

The next large traditional temple you reach along the river bank is the triple-roofed **Tripura Sundari**, which was built in 1818 at the request of Queen Tripura Sundari, the wife of Rana Bahadur Shah, to increase her own religious merit. The temple stands on a broad pedestal with small temples at each corner containing members of the Panchayana deities. The supporting roof struts illustrate figures in the *Mahabharata* epic (see pages 108–9).

Along the Ghats, as far as Pachali, is an assortment of temples of different sizes. One unusual group consists of three *shikharas* grouped over a single sanctum; this was probably built during the late 19th century.

At the end of the river bank is a further cluster of *shikharas* and temples, together with the cremation platforms. Although little research has been carried out in this area, it is believed that several of the temples are of early foundation and an early *chaitya*, possibly of the Licchavi period, has been located.

Singha Durbar and Other Palaces

The Singha Durbar, the most spectacular Rana palace in Kathmandu, was constructed in 1901. It is considered to be one of the largest private dwellings of its kind, and originally consisted of seven courtyards and over 1,000 rooms. Although it was severely damaged by fire in 1973, much has been rebuilt behind the magnificent front elevation. There are several other palaces near the Singha Durbar on the eastern side of Kathmandu.

To complete a short tour of the Rana palaces it is worth visiting the **Hari Bhawan**, located near the sports stadium. One of the oldest palace estates and now government offices, it was built by Prime Minister Bhimsen Thapa in 1805. It was originally known as **Bagh Durbar** because live tigers were caged at its entrance. It acquired its present name in 1940 when it was occupied and renovated by Hari Shamsher.

Environs of Kathmandu

Swayambhu

Swayambhu, the Buddhist shrine set on a hillock to the west of Kathmandu, is reputedly the oldest settlement in the Kathmandu Valley. There are two ways of reaching it: either along the pilgrims' route across the river from Kathmandu and up the narrow and steep stairway on the eastern side of the hillock, or by a road, recently constructed, which arrives at a point on the saddle of the hill beneath the shrine and only a short distance from it. The walk from the centre of Kathmandu takes about half an hour.

The founding of Swayambhu is shrouded in legend. It is said that the Kathmandu Valley was formerly a lake upon which no lotus grew. Vipssaya Buddha, many aeons ago, threw a root of the lotus on to the lake and then recited charms over it, saying 'When this lotus shall flower, Swayambhu, or the Self-Existent One, shall be revealed as a flame.' Much later, Visvabhu Buddha prophesied the prosperity of the Valley as soon as a Bodhisattva should cause the land to appear above the waters. It was then that Manjusri, assuming the form of Visvakarma, smote with his sword an enclosing hill on the southern edge of the Valley and drained the lake by way of the Bagmati River, through what today is known as Chobar Gorge. Swayambhu thus came into being and a shrine was built on the hill to protect the lotus.

Though much altered, the Swayambhu *stupa* today overlooks the Valley, surrounded by several smaller shrines and temples. There is also a Tibetan monastery, which was established in its present form in the 1950s, though it is said to have been founded much earlier.

The dome of the *stupa* is of the same low, flat type characteristic of the others to be found in the Valley. The *stupa* itself stands upon a large platform, constructed presumably by levelling off the top of the hill, which falls away steeply on all sides. The eastern approach road is guarded towards its summit by pairs of animals—garudas, peacocks, horses, elephants and lions—all being vehicles of the Five Buddhas. At the top of the stairway is an enormous 1.5-metre (five-foot) -long *vajra*, or thunderbolt, a symbol of sacred power. It rests upon a *mandala*, and around the drum are cut the symbols of the Tibetan calendar. The eyes of supreme Buddhahood peer down from the base of the pinnacle over the dome, while above towers the great gilded pinnacle with its 13 rings and crowning parasol. Around the main shrine, gilt figures dedicated to the Five Divine Buddhas are set in iron-curtained shrines. In a recess beneath each figure is depicted the beast or bird sacred to the Buddha. Very close to the *stupa* is an important shrine, the **Harati Ajima**, a two-tiered temple of Hindu influence containing an image of Bhagbati. The temple is clad almost entirely in gilded copper with very fine detailing. According to local people, the main deity in this temple protects children from disease, especially smallpox, and it is common for

mothers to bring their new-born babies here for 'immunization'.

Flanking the steps are two imposing *shikhara*-style shrines. The one to the north was built by Pratap Malla in 1654, and the one to the south at the same time by Ananta Priyadevi, one of his queens. Around and about the platform to the *stupa* are several hundred small *chaityas* and votive offerings, among which are some early Licchavi relics. Set into a recently constructed brick surround is one of the finest stone statues of the standing Buddha. It is considered one of the oldest statues of its kind in Nepal and dates from the ninth or tenth century. Taking the northern route down from the stupa you will pass another impressive seated Buddha from the same period.

Opposite there is an uninspiring single-storeyed building known as **Shantipur**. In contrast to its appearance, the history of this building is intriguing. It is said that a certain Gunkamadeva displeased the gods by committing incest and so they caused a drought and famine. To appease the gods, the nine *nags* or serpents were brought under the control of Gunkamadeva with the help of Shantikar, who was living in the temple and from whom the temple derives its name. The *nags* worshipped him and each gave him a likeness of himself drawn with his own blood, declaring that whenever there was a drought, plentiful, rain would fall as soon as these pictures were worshipped. Even today, in times of severe drought, the king will, as a final resort, visit this shrine to pray for rain.

In August 1979 the Swayambhu hillock was ravaged by a landslip caused by very heavy rains. A section of the southeastern corner of the site, close to the Pratapur *shikhara*, slid down the hill, threatening further devastation to the *stupa* itself. A team from the Hanuman Dhoka Project undertook a very tricky but successful drainage programme around the susceptible zone and new viewing platforms overlooking Kathmandu were created. The major cause for concern was that the foundations of the tall *shikhara* would fail, but investigations proved that these had been built directly off the bedrock forming the crown of the hillock. The brick foundation was eight metres (25 feet) deep—a massive structure indeed. During excavations a unique and intact stone sculpture of Padmapani Avaloketeswar was found in one of the trenches at a depth of two and a half metres (eight feet). It is said to be one of the earliest intact sculptures to have been found, possibly dating from the sixth century. It can be seen in the small sculpture museum at the head of the steps from the car park.

On the western slopes of the Swayambhu hill are several other shrines, including a small *chaitya* sacred to Manjusri, who is identified with his partner Saraswati. They are worshipped by both Hindus and Buddhists, making this one of the main national shrines of Nepal.

The siting of Swayambhu is magnificent. There are wonderful views over Kathmandu as well as the Valley and, on a clear day, the sunset over the hills and snow peaks in the distance is indescribably beautiful.

Sites to the East of Kathmandu

The following sites are to the east of Kathmandu and all are within a short taxi ride of one another. For those using a bicycle, there are short-cuts through the back streets. Take a good map to help you find your way.

Pashupatinath and Gujeswari

The Pashupatinath and Gujeswari sites constitute the largest temple group in the Valley, and cover an extended area on both sides of the Bagmati River. The shrine of Pashupatinath is one of the holiest Hindu shrines in all Nepal. Set on the banks of the Bagmati, one of the major uses of this religious centre is as a place where the souls of dying people can be released by laying them with their feet in the river; after death their mortal remains are cremated on the river bank.

Pashupatinath is also the scene of several colourful festivals throughout the year (see pages 167–75) as well as a place for constant individual worship. Despite the continuous activity on the river banks and around the temple there is always a sense of peace and tranquillity here.

The present **temple to Shiva Pashupati**, lord of the animals and protector of the Valley, dates from 1696, but its history goes back to the beginning of the 15th century. The present temple was constructed by Birpalendra Malla after the former structure had been severely damaged by termites. Throughout its history there have been so many additions and so much refurbishing that it is now difficult to tell how much of the original structure survives. The roofs and the pediments over the main doors are of gilded copper and the doors themselves are of repoussé silverwork of very fine quality. The main entrance to the shrine, along the road from the west, is distinguished by the rear end of a gigantic golden bull—that of Nandi, Shiva's celestial vehicle. The inner sanctum contains several fine images and shrines donated by important and wealthy worshippers. Access is strictly limited to Hindus, but it is possible to get a view of the temple precincts from the other side of the river.

Take a path along the side of the complex and along the west bank of the Bagmati; you will find an amazing collection of **stone sculptures**, some of them dating from the fifth century, as well as a collection of small shrines. Many of the sculptures and shrines are of Buddhist origin. Set back from the river on the west side are courtyard buildings which house the poor.

Crossing the river by the upstream bridge you can see the two large **cremation platforms** directly beneath the main temple, used only by the royal family and prime ministers. On the opposite bank are other votive shrines and another complex of courtyards, where pilgrims lodge during the big festivals. Continuing up this long flight of stone-paved stairs you come to a peaceful area known as **Gujeswari**, which is set in a wooded glade. The main temple on the upper level is a *shikhara*, dedicated to Goraknath. The *shikhara* was built in the 18th century and houses a footprint of Goraknath.

Below this group there is the **temple of Gujeswari**, the shrine of the spouse of Shiva in her manifestation as Kali. Its date of construction is not known but the first recorded repairs were made by Pratap Malla in the 17th century. Access to this shrine is also limited to Hindus. To itemize and identify all the beautiful religious works of art to be found in this temple complex would take too long and be too difficult, but most of the important examples will speak for themselves.

Chabahil

Returning to the main road and continuing in the direction of Baudhanath, it is worth stopping a while at Chabahil, the small *stupa* located on the west of the road before you enter the next village. The village known as Chabahil is a very early settlement containing two important *behals*, the Ganesh shrine protecting Pashupati and the *stupa* reckoned to be of the third century BC and therefore one of the earliest in the Valley. It has legendary associations with King Brishadev, and there is a story that it was built with the remains of the materials excavated during the construction of Baudhanath. There are several early classical stone sculptures, including at one time an exquisite standing Buddha of the ninth century, which was recently stolen, and an interesting stone image of Manjusri set in a small brick construction. Around the base of the *stupa* itself is an interesting collection of stone carvings, including images of horses and female devotees. In a stucco building to the north of the *stupa* is a large seated Buddha of unknown origin with a small aperture beneath it. Local belief has it that if you can crawl through this opening you are never guilty of telling lies.

The Chabahil and **Kuti Bahal** are located at the back of the *stupa*. Little remains of their former beauty, but according to legend Chabahil Bahal was founded by Charumati, the daughter of King Ashoka. The way there is difficult to describe but any of the local people will lead you to them.

Baudhanath

On the outskirts of Chabahil, you will have your first glimpse of the massive Baudhanath *stupa*, which rises out of the paddy fields against the brilliant blue sky and the backdrop of the snow peaks of the Himalaya. This is truly one of the great sights in the Kathmandu Valley. At first, it is not possible to relate its size to anything tangible, but gradually the encircling dwellings become apparent. When you arrive at the entrance to the *stupa* you feel dwarfed by its size and there is nowhere around the *stupa* where you can stand back and take it in as a whole. Once you have started on the circumambulation of the shrine you will be distracted by the trinket shops and the children who congregate around this centre of pilgrimage. Baudhanath has always been a trading centre and the shops that now sell souvenirs were formerly owned and run by Newari goldsmiths and silversmiths who traded with Tibet. Tibetans used to travel, as they still do today, from the mountains to trade and barter during the major festivals, thus combining business with pilgrimage. On the western side of the *stupa* there are still lodging houses for itinerant hillmen, more especially those from the Gurung settlements.

Of the traditional **Newari goldsmiths' shops**, only one still survives in its original form and that is on the eastern corner. Newari traders, especially silversmiths, are still to be found near the gateway to the *stupa* itself, doing traditional silver repoussé work. Unfortunately, most of the original buildings have been superseded by ugly concrete boxes.

The origin of the *stupa* is a little obscure. It is reputed that it was built by a girl of supernatural birth called Kangma who was guilty of stealing flowers from Indra's heaven. As punishment she was reborn as the daughter of a swineherd in the Kathmandu Valley. She married, had four children and was widowed. Left to her own devices, she became a goose girl and accumulated a fortune from her labours. She wanted to build a noble temple to Buddha Amitabha and requested the king to give her as much ground as the hide of a buffalo would cover. The king agreed and the girl cut the hide into thin strips and joined them together. Stretching the thongs out to form a square she claimed—and in spite of local jealousies, was given—the land on which she commenced building the Baudhanath *stupa*. After her death, her sons completed it and placed in it some relics of Kasyapa Buddha. Over the centuries the basic form of the *stupa* has been altered. Today, the dome is set on a platform in the shape of a *mandala* and supports a finely proportioned pinnacle which, unlike that at Swayambhu, is square in section. The dome and its base are whitewashed and have a design in yellow paint which simulates the lotus. During major festivals, hundreds of prayer flags are draped from the pinnacle to the perimeter of the platform. The enclosing wall around the stupa is studded with hundreds of prayer wheels that are spun by the faithful as they promenade round and round the *stupa*.

As at Swayambhu, at the entrance to the *stupa* itself there is an image of Chwaskamini Ajima in silver plate set in a small shrine. Behind the shrine there is a splendid over-lifesize prayer wheel and alongside it there are some interesting images, some of which are of Hindu origin.

To get a brief insight into the Buddhist way of life, it is worth visiting one of the many **new monasteries in Baudhanath** that have sprung up around the stupa. Most of them follow a standard pattern of layout. An open porch leads into the principal chapel, with the main altar containing the divinities facing the entrance. The chapel is usually square in plan and generally about eight metres (25 feet) square. The heavy ceiling structure and roof are supported by four centrally placed pillars with heavy, carved cantilever brackets. The interior is usually rather dark and an air of tranquillity pervades. Despite the lack of light, the pillars are ornately painted with scenes from the life of the Buddha. The pillars and brackets are embossed and embellished with gold paint and the ceiling is painted in vivid colours. The chapels are always spotlessly clean and visitors are welcome at all times. If possible, you should visit such a monastery during one of the daily prayer recitals, as it is only then that the true atmosphere can be felt.

Dhum Varahi

When returning, if you take the new ring road from Chabahil in the direction of Maharajgunj, you will be able to visit one of the oldest shrines in the Valley—the Dhum Varahi, which is located on the left side of the road, a short distance after the bridge over the Dhobikhola River. This sixth-century sculpture set in a small brick shrine is of Vishnu in his incarnation as the boar. He assumed this disguise to destroy the demon Hiranyaksha who was pulling the earth under water. It is a life-size image of great beauty and it is remarkable that a piece of such fine quality should be found in such a remote area. It can only suggest that there was an important settlement here at some time in the past.

Budhanilkantha

The next place to visit is Budhanilkantha, which can be reached via Maharajgunj, on a road leading north out of Kathmandu. If you continue along the ring road and take the next turning north after this last stop you will be going in the right direction. Budhanilkantha lies beneath the hill of Shivapuri and at the northernmost extremity of the Valley. It is another representation of Vishnu, reputedly dating from the fifth century. The image depicts Vishnu reclining on a bed of snakes, fast asleep as a result of having drunk a draught of poison. The image, which is said to be carved out of a single block of stone, is set in a pool, thus giving it the appearance of floating. During the local festival of Baikuntha Chaturdasi in November, thousands of people from all over the Valley flock to pay homage to Vishnu at this site.

Until the recent development of a large boarding school complex close to the shrine, Budhanilkantha was remote from the rest of the Valley. Much of its charm and character have been lost with a major restoration of the compound. An ancient pipal tree, which used to shade the image and pilgrims alike, was felled, and the finest of all sculptures in the Valley has been imprisoned by an ugly concrete fence.

If there is still time available, it is worth while continuing along the road and driving up to the former isolation hospital above the new school. From here there are magnificent views over the Valley.

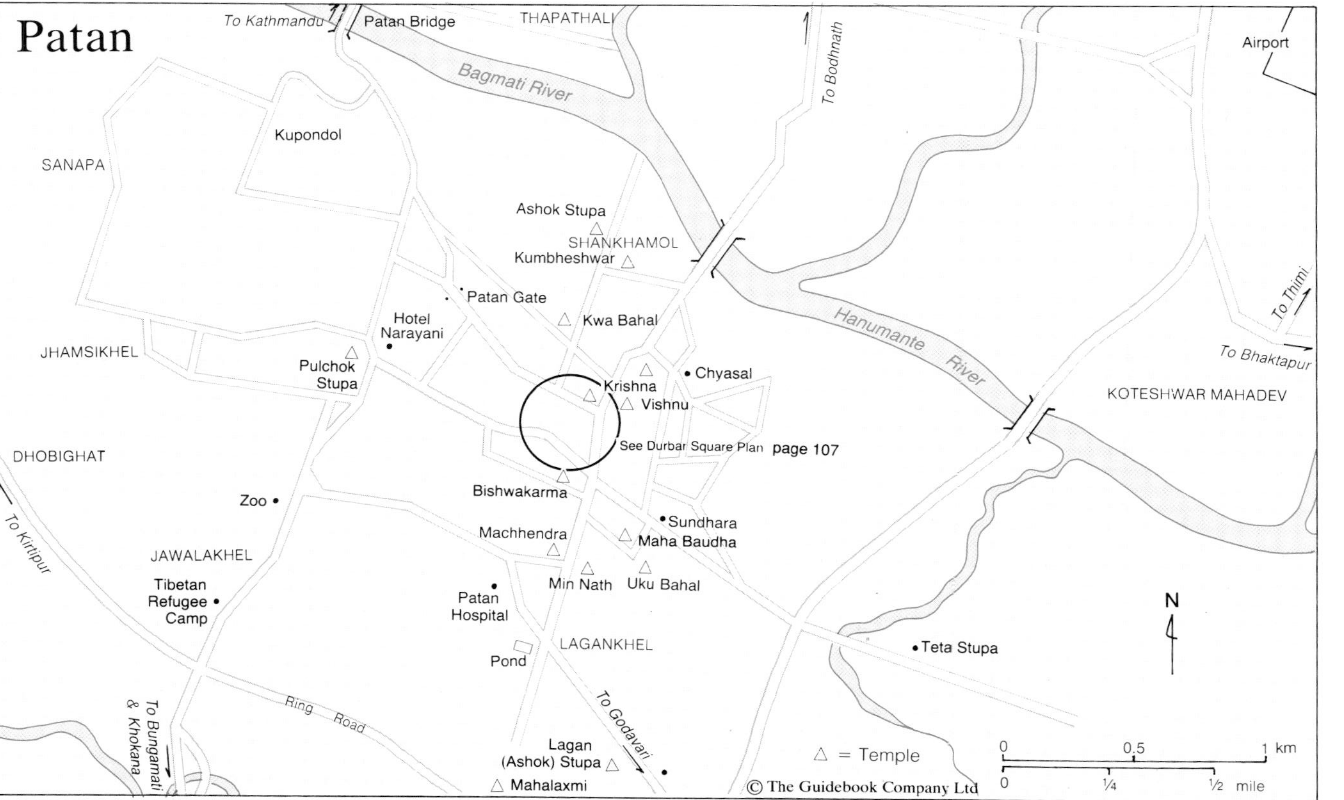
Patan
To Kathmandu
Patan Bridge
THAPATHALI
Bagmati River
To Bodhnath
Airport
Kupondol
SANAPA
Ashok Stupa
SHANKHAMOL
Kumbheshwar
Patan Gate
Kwa Bahal
Hotel Narayani
JHAMSIKHEL
Pulchok Stupa
Hanumante River
To Thimi
To Bhaktapur
Chyasal
Krishna
Vishnu
KOTESHWAR MAHADEV
DHOBIGHAT
See Durbar Square Plan page 107
Bishwakarma
Zoo
To Kirtipur
Sundhara
Machhendra
Maha Baudha
JAWALAKHEL
Min Nath
Uku Bahal
Tibetan Refugee Camp
Patan Hospital
N
LAGANKHEL
Teta Stupa
Pond
Ring Road
To Bungamati & Khokana
To Godavari
Lagan (Ashok) Stupa
Mahalaxmi
△ = Temple
0
0.5
1 km
0
¼
½ mile
© The Guidebook Company Ltd

Patan

The Road to Patan

Patan or Lalitpur—the Beautiful City, as it is often called—lies to the southeast of Kathmandu. Originally the towns were separated by the Bagmati River and a swathe of paddy fields between. Patan, being on slightly higher ground than Kathmandu, overlooks the river and the surrounding countryside and the views towards the Himalaya are truly spectacular. Because of the expansion of these two cities, right down to the river banks, the demarcation between them is now only the river, and the Patan bridge provides the main vehicular access point between the two cities.

The distance between the two durbar squares is about seven kilometres (four miles) and normally the journey by taxi costs about Rs50. However, Patan can easily be reached by bicycle. It takes about 20 minutes to tackle the moderate hills leading to its outskirts. If you take the main road towards Jawalakhel, you pass some fine-looking Rana palaces—now government offices—on the left-hand side before you reach the Narayani Hotel. Just a few hundred metres (yards) above the hotel on the right you will notice a grassy mound. This is west of the four Ashoka *stupas* that are placed at the cardinal points around Patan. At this point you turn left (east) along a road that serves as the main access to the Durbar Square. The road narrows to run between terraced houses with overhanging roofs garlanded with vegetables hanging from the eaves to dry. As you look to your left and right you will notice small openings either under or between buildings that open into small courtyards beyond, and this will give you an idea of the many hundreds of courtyards, or *bahals*, that make up the network of dwellings in Patan. You enter the Durbar Square at its southwestern extremity to behold one of the great architectural vistas in the Kathmandu Valley, culminating in the snowcapped Langtang peak in the distance.

A Tour through the Patan Durbar Square

As in the Kathmandu Durbar Square, there are very fine buildings of religious and royal foundation centred on the Patan royal palace. The Patan Durbar Square is smaller than that of Kathmandu; nevertheless it contains some very special buildings. As the palace is no longer occupied as an official residence, it is possible to visit all the courtyards and therefore to get some idea of what those inaccessible areas in the Hanuman Dhoka are like. Unlike the latter, the *chowks*, or courtyards, of Patan are not interconnecting. Each *chowk* is accessible from the main road along which they are strung, and at the rear they lead through narrow doorways to the former palace garden. On the opposite side of the road to the palace are some interesting temples, mostly founded by royal patronage.

The Patan Durbar Square is located in the very heart of the city, at the meeting-point of the two trading routes, now known as **Mangal Bazaar**. The open square containing the palace and the temples is delineated by a boundary of irregular-shaped dwellings. All the temples located in this open square are set facing the entrance to the palace, even though there was no predetermined layout. Most of them were built by royalty in memory of their respective parents and their religious importance varies because of this. However, each building records an element of the historical development of this Durbar Square.

The palace courtyards, which appear to have been built as separate units following traditional plans, are of typical construction, but have no regard for the neighbouring structures. No existing building in the palace dates before the 17th century, although the present structures probably stand on almost the identical foundations of earlier buildings or even replace them. The palace took its present form largely during the reign of Siddhi Narasingha Malla and Shrinivasa Malla, who reigned between 1620 and 1660 and between 1660 and 1684 respectively.

Sundari Chowk, the most southerly courtyard and the first you come to, was completed in 1627 and was designed as the residence of Siddhi Narasingha and his family. At the same time, the **Tusa Hiti**, the beautiful bathing tank and water-spout, were built in the centre of the courtyard. The octagonal form of this tank was to emphasize the king's devotion to the eight *nags*, the goddesses of rain. The inner walls of the tank are lined with hundreds of deities in stone and metal, consisting of the ten matrikas, the ten bhairabs, the ten nagas, as well as the Dashavatar of Vishnu, in fact all the favourite gods of the king. The water-spout itself is a gilded conch shell and the water was originally piped from the surrounding hills. The perimeter of the tank is surrounded by a pair of serpents carved in stone. At the entrance to the bath is a stone slab raised off the ground, which was used by the king as a throne for meditation. The courtyard is enclosed by a three-storeyed building with exquisitely carved details in the windows, doors and other decorative elements. These would have been the living-quarters of the king and his family.

You will notice that, as in Kathmandu, the main entrance to this courtyard is guarded by images of Narasingha, Hanuman and Ganesh. The central window over the door is of gilded metal and is flanked by windows decorated in ivory. Even the name, Sundari (beautiful) Chowk, given it by Siddhi Narasingha hardly does justice to the magnificence of this little courtyard.

The next courtyard is the **Mul Chowk**, completed in 1660. It is probable that Siddhi Narasingha commenced its construction and that it was completed by his successor Shrinivasa as a dedication to the goddess Durga. However, the deity Mantraju, for which the small central gilded sanctuary, the **Bidya Temple**, was erected, was the favourite house goddess of the ruler. Shortly afterwards, Shrinivasa Malla erected a temple for the Agamdevta, or secret house goddess, in the south wing of the courtyard, which is still guarded by the life-size figures of Ganga and Yamuna in gilded bronze. Over the shrine is a three-tiered roof. What remains of the beautiful metal doorway at the entrance of the shrine is indeed a tribute to the metalworkers for which Patan is still famous. As in the Hanuman Dhoka Palace, the Patan Mul Chowk is a low, two-storeyed building housing the priests who officiated in the palace. Although much altered in recent years, it still retains its carved supporting roof struts depicting Bhairabs and Matrikas. Much of their beauty, however, is masked by the thick layers of paint covering them. In the northeastern corner there is the **Taleju Temple**, which was built by Shrinivasa Malla and completed in 1671. It was erected over the three-storeyed palace building and consists of a three-tiered roof, the corners of which have been cut off to give it the impression of having an octagonal form. This building can be entered only by the priests responsible for the worship of the deity.

Because the courtyard was used as a gathering place for various religious dances and ceremonies, you will notice that the doors are much larger than usual. The entrance is guarded by two stone lions.

Adjacent to the Mul Chowk and dominating the palace complex because of its size is the **Degutaleju Temple**, again constructed by Siddhi Narsingha in 1641. It was originally a four-storeyed building, although it reached five storeys before it was destroyed by fire. It is built off a part of the palace and has a triple-tiered roof structure. The temple is dedicated to Taleju Bhawani, and is inaccessible to all but the priests. There is a special room built on the orders of the king where he could retire for prayers, meditation and the recitation of *mantras*.

The third courtyard of the palace complex, now occupied by a museum, is the **Keshab Narayan Chowk**. This is the main palace building and the last of the courtyards to be completed. It took about 60 years to build, starting in the reign of Shrinivasa Malla, and was dedicated by his successor, Shrivishnu, in 1734. To facilitate this extension of the palace, it was necessary to remove the adjacent Buddhist monastery known as Hakhusi Bahal, which caused difficulties of a mainly religious nature. The *bahal* was duly removed and rebuilt close by. Since then, on the occasion of certain Buddhist festivals, an image of Lord Buddha, encased in a square copper container, is placed in front of the main door where it is the object of great devotion.

The inner courtyard façades have succumbed to the results of poor alterations and restoration. The external elevation, however, is of exceptional beauty and well worth close study. It is probable that the projecting balconies and the central gilded window were added to the lower storeys by Shrivishnu Malla and erected, according to the chronicles, in three months. Although these windows are coated in dirt and paint, it is possible to visualize the intricacy of the carvings. The central gilded window is one of the finest of its kind and it is here that the kings would sit to look out over their subjects and

gaze upon the Krishna Temple.

The Keshab Narayan Chowk has undergone partial conservation under the guidance of the Hanuman Dhoka Conservation Team. It was discovered that this structure had undergone several reconstructions subsequent to the damage it sustained in the 1934 earthquake. The latest work was as recent as the early 1970s when the interior balconies were remodelled. After exhaustive research, the team was able to ascertain from a collection of early photographs, that the former silhouette of the upper floors was completely different and, by carefully extrapolating measurements from the photographs, it was and by carefully extrapolating measurements from the photographs, it was able to reconstruct the roofs and corner turrets to match the original. Recently the courtyard buildings have been remodelled, with modern intrusions, to house the original museum collection.

Leaving the Keshab Narayan Chowk, the building opposite—the magnificent Krishna Temple—will be the first to catch your eye. It was the favourite of its builder, Siddhi Narasingha Malla, who completed it in 1637, having taken six years to construct it. It is one of only a few buidings in stone and contains some very delicate relief carvings of the two epics, the *Ramayana* and the *Mahabharata*, around the lintels above the collonade. The temple is of the *shikhara* style and the tower only emerges after the second storey. It is set on a stone plinth and the lower floor to the shrine is arcaded. The actual sanctum is on the first floor which is formed, as is the second level, of a series of smaller pavilions capped with pinnacles. Take a moment to study the friezes depicting the epics. Although to all but the scholar it is difficult at first to separate one from the other, the individual tableaux are graphically illustrated and follow in sequence in a clockwise direction, rather like a cartoon strip.

On the northern perimeter of this open space and adjacent to the Krishna Mandir is a large two-tiered temple with a pair of guardian elephants, one on either side of the entrance to the sanctuary. This is the **Bishwanath Temple**, built in 1626 by Siddhi Narasingha. It is of unusual form in that, around the inner sanctum, it has an arcade of finely carved timber pillars which are supported by carved stone stills. Above each pair of pillars there are ornately carved *toranas* depicting various divinities or aspects of Shiva. The supporting carved roof struts figure Ganesh, Surya—the sun god, Annapurna, and Shiva with Parvati. It is one of the earlier temples in the Durbar Square and merits a closer look than most.

Close by and further to the north is another large building, the **temple to Bhimsen**, which is one of the most important in the square. Like the Bhimsen Temple in Kathmandu, it is a centre for worship especially for local businessmen. The sanctuary is on the upper floor and is lit by a large balconied window over the entrance door. The temple was built under royal patronage by Shrinivasa Malla and completed in 1681. Although it has been 'modern-

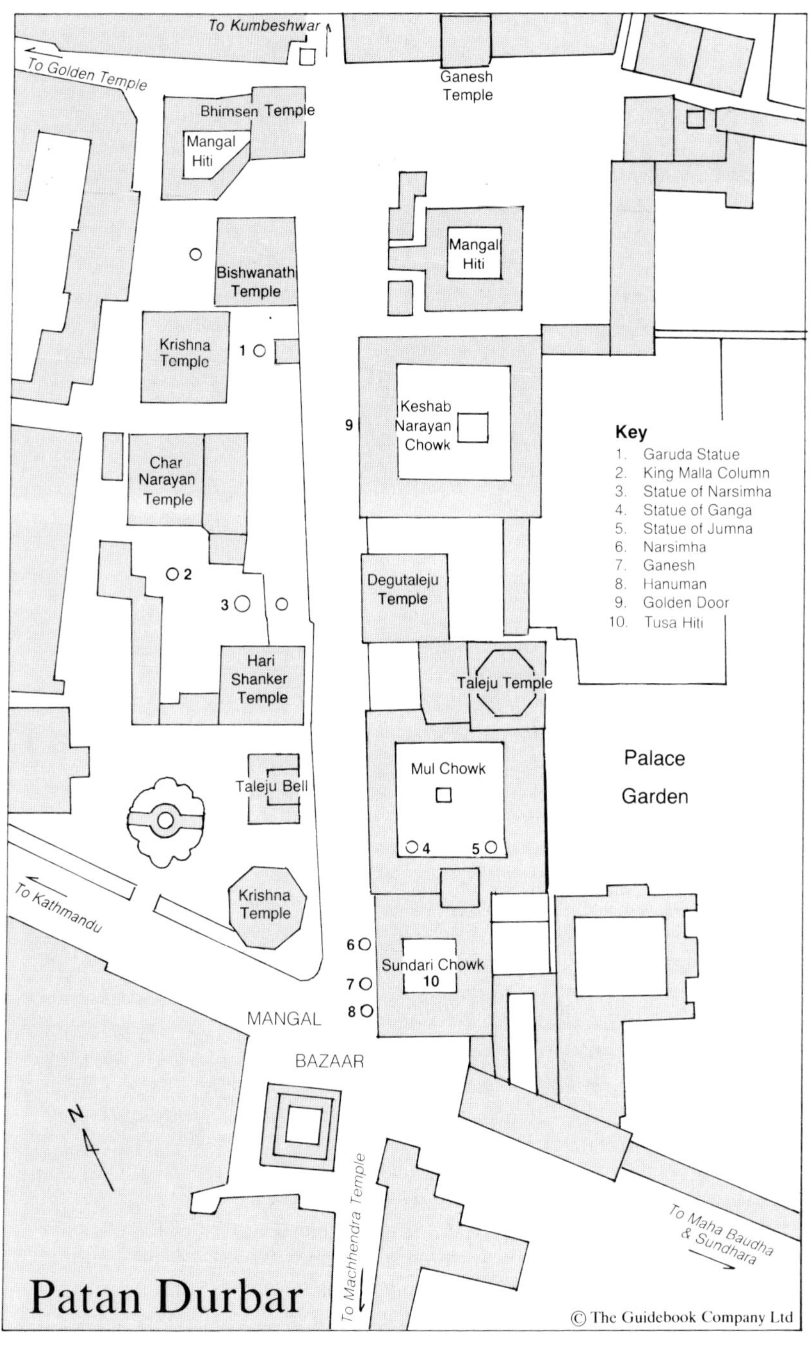

To Kumbeshwar
To Golden Temple
Ganesh Temple
Bhimsen Temple
Mangal Hiti
Mangal Hiti
Bishwanath Temple
Krishna Temple
1
Keshab Narayan Chowk
9
Key
1. Garuda Statue
2. King Malla Column
3. Statue of Narsimha
4. Statue of Ganga
5. Statue of Jumna
6. Narsimha
7. Ganesh
8. Hanuman
9. Golden Door
10. Tusa Hiti
Char Narayan Temple
2
3
Degutaleju Temple
Hari Shanker Temple
Taleju Temple
Mul Chowk
Palace Garden
Taleju Bell
4
5
To Kathmandu
Krishna Temple
6
Sundari Chowk
10
7
8
MANGAL
BAZAAR
N
To Machhendra Temple
To Maha Baudha & Sundhara
Patan Durbar

The Mahabharata

by Kakoli Thompson

The *Mahabharata*, with its 100,000 verses, is thought to be the longest epic poem in the world. Historically, it is accredited to the Indian sage, Veda Vyasa, a relative of the main protagonists and observer of the events. The core was composed in the fifth or fourth century BC, but it was added to until at least the fourth century AD.

The main story concerns a feud between two royal clans, the Pandavas and their cousins, the Kauravas. The Kauravas are the hundred sons of King Dhritarashtra. The Pandavas are his five nephews: Yudisthira, Bhima, Arjuna, Nakula and Sahadeva, for whom he has acted as regent since their own father's death. The Kauravas, bitterly jealous of their cousins since childhood, are especially so when Dhritarashtra makes Yudisthira his heir.

When Yudhisthira comes of age, his cousin, Duryodhana, persuades his father to let him succeed instead and to agree to a plot to kill the Pandavas. But the Pandavas are warned in time and flee to the forest with their mother, Kunti.

While in the forest, the Pandavas hear of an archery contest for the hand of the Princess Draupadi. They attend the contest and Arjuna wins. Delighted, he tells his mother, on returning to the forest, that he has won a great prize. Before Arjuna can tell her what the prize entails, however, she insists that he share it with his brothers. This is how Draupadi became the wife of all five brothers.

The Kauravas eventually decide to divide their kingdom into two and the Pandavas accept the invitation to go home. But peace is shortlived. The ambitious Duryodhana begins to plot against his cousins again, and, knowing Yudhisthira's weakness, challenges him to a game of dice. Yudhisthira loses everything he has, from his kingdom to his brothers and Draupadi.

The unfortunate princess is molested by Duryodhana and one of his brothers, but mercifully the gods intervene; the tables turn and Draupadi demands her family's freedom. But Yudhisthira once again accepts Duryodhana's challenge to another game of dice and, once again, loses. This time, the Pandavas have to go into a 12-year exile in the forest. At the end of their exile, the Pandavas wage war as Duryodhana continues to deny his cousins their rightful share of the kingdom.

On the field of Kurukshetra a heroic battle is fought. It is on the eve of this battle that the poem reaches its climax in the great *Bhagvadgita*, or celestial song, delivered to Arjuna by his charioteer—an incarnation of Lord Krishna, the supreme being. To most Hindus, this sermon forms their main religious text and is the source of many of their beliefs.

Arjuna has decided to refuse to fight his relatives. Krishna argues with him by teaching that the soul, being eternal and indestructible, does not die when the body is killed, but transmigrates from body to body until it achieves final release. He applies this to Arjuna's own situation, declaring that since death is not final, there is no need for sorrow over the deaths that are imminent in battle. Krishna then expounds the view that all activity is a sacrifice if undertaken in the right spirit—one of complete detachment. He explains that, just as he himself, as the supreme deity, has no need to act but is incessantly engaged in activity, since otherwise the universe would collapse, so men should help to maintain the world order by sacrificially motivated activity. Thus, Arjuna should perform his duty of fighting the enemy, but in a spirit of complete detachment, without concern for the outcome.

Arjuna fights. After many heroic struggles, the Kaurava forces and, finally, Duryodhana himself, are defeated. The triumphant Pandavas return to the ancestral kingdom and Yudhisthira ascends the throne.

But another tragedy befalls them: Dhritarashtra and two wives, including the Pandavas' mother, are killed in a forest fire. Yudhisthira renounces the throne, and the five brothers and Draupadi make a pilgrimage. After many trials and tests, they find peace at last and enter heaven triumphant.

ized' by the application of glazed tiles and silver paint to the lower carvings, there are still some fine carvings to be seen. For example, on the southern elevation, a wooden panel narrates episodes from Bhimsen's life. The topmost of the three tiers of roof is covered in gilded metal and has a fine set of finials; from the centre of this roof falls a metal ribbon-like banner with *mantras* engraved on it, given by a wealthy benefactor. The temple is open for worship every day, but is especially popular on Tuesdays and Saturdays.

Directly opposite the entrance to the Bhimsen Temple is perhaps the oldest physical structure in the Patan Durbar Square—the **Mangal Hiti**—an important water conduit which was originally excavated in the tenth century, during the Lichhavi period. This tank is now at least four metres (13 feet) below the present street level and still provides a good source of water which pours from the mouths of three stone crocodiles. There are also images of Lakshminarayan and Barume set into the walls of the conduit.

At the southern perimeter of this space in front of the Keshab Narayan Chowk is the large three-tiered and arcaded **temple to Hari Shanker**, built by Siddhi Narasingha in the 17th century. The size of this temple is important. It acts as a stop to the southern end of the square, as the temples and bell beyond are of less importance to the square's overall environment. The kneeling elephants at the entrance to the sanctum and the exquisitely carved *toranas* are noteworthy.

Somewhat dwarfed by the Hari Shanker Temple is a small two-tiered temple of great historical importance, the **Char Narayan Temple**. It was built in 1566 by Purandharsingha and there is an inscription recording his setting up images of Narayan and his four attendants. The style of building characteristic of these early temples is well represented here. Its proportions are squat with a dominating set of roofs; the angle of the brackets is flatter, but perhaps the most dominant features on all four elevations are the heavy doors and flanking windows with simple sills and frames. These doorways lead into an inner circumambulatory around a central stone *lingam* representing the deity.

On the southern edge of the Durbar Square itself, the unusual octagonal stone **temple to Krishna**, completed in 1723, is worth looking at. There are a few traditional temples with an octagonal plan but this is the only stone building of its kind. Although plain in decoration, its design was no doubt influenced by the Mughal architecture of India. It was built by Yogamati, Yogendra Malla's daughter, after the death of her father and son Lokaprakasha, to gain merit for them in their next life.

Places to Discover in Patan

There are two walks around Patan that can be combined into one but, as they are on either side of the Durbar Square, they have been covered separately here.

North Patan: Kumbheswar and Kwa Bahal

Taking the northern route out of the Patan Durbar Square, leaving the Bhimsen Temple on your left, you enter a typical streetscape that is narrow to begin with before widening out into a small open square. The large building on the left is a temple dedicated to Krishna. It is a well-proportioned three-tiered structure with fine roof struts depicting the incarnations of Vishnu.

The little two-tiered temple on the right is worth a closer look, if only to see the fine Garuda image which was donated in 1706, the *nag* or snake set into the paving, and the beautiful stone image of the four-armed Vishnu in the shrine.

The street narrows again and you can see the original paving of the road and the open drainage system. An opening to the right contains an insignificant two-tiered shrine known as **Uma Maheswar.** However, inside this shrine there is one of the most beautiful stone carvings of the tenth century, a representation of Shiva and his consort Parvati. Beneath them, an inscription records the sculpture's creation.

About 40 metres (yards) beyond, a turning to the left leads down a paved street which formerly had two lines of fine terraced houses typifying the traditional Newari town house. As the street opens out to your right you can see the beautiful **Kumbheswar Temple** towering above the surrounding houses.

Kumbheswar is located within its own complex of resthouses, small shrines and a tank. The main temple, with its magnificent five tiers of diminishing roofs, is reckoned to be the oldest temple in Patan, although today its form is very different to what it was originally. It was built in 1392, during the reign of Jayastithi Malla, when the temple was referred to as two-tiered. It was during the reign of Shrinivasa Malla, 1660–84, that the upper three roofs were added, making it one of two major temples in the Valley with five roofs. The temple itself is very delicate in design but the two lower roofs have similar proportions to that of the Char Narayan (see page 110). The supporting roof struts, the windows and doors are all heavily carved and are very beautiful but in poor condition. The inner sanctum contains a very striking gilded silver *lingam*. Originally this temple had a traditional tiled roof, but some over-zealous politicians removed the tiles and replaced them with costly copper sheeting, which ruins the texture as well as the proportion of an otherwise unique religious compound.

In the compound there are several interesting smaller shrines of varying ages and importance. Several of these are of Lichhavi origin, making this part of Patan one of the earliest parts of the city. It is a very important site for religious festivals, the main festival being the Kumbheswar Mela during Janai Purnima.

One of the earliest Buddhist *stupas* in Patan is located just behind Kumbheswar. Taking a right-hand turn out of the back gate of the compound beneath the enormous pipal tree, the road leads round to the left. Follow this for a few hundred metres (yards) and the *stupa* will be visible on the left. This is one of five believed to have been built by Ashoka, the Mauryan king of India, while on a visit to Nepal. Thus it can be dated to the third century BC. Unlike the *stupas* on the other tour, this *stupa* has been plastered over, but it is certain to have been a fairly recent alteration. There are several good Buddhist sculptures within the compound.

Retracing your tracks to Kumbheswar, take the direct but narrower road into the city between further good examples of town dwellings. After the road widens, you will see on your right a small entrance guarded by a pair of temple lions. This is the entrance to the **Kwa Bahal**, one of the most spectacular of the many hundreds of Buddhist monasteries to be found in and around Patan. Often referred to as Hirana Varna Mahavihar, this monastery was founded in 1409 and is dedicated to Gautama Buddha. The whole façade of the main temple enshrining the Buddha and the roofs is covered with embossed gilded copper. The metalwork, especially of the *toranas*, is very detailed and finely executed. The small shrine in the centre of the courtyard is lavishly embellished with metal designs and figures, all of which merit a closer look. You will notice that many details are of strong Hindu influence. The crowning pinnacle, or *gajur*, to this shrine is very ornate indeed and, although a little top-heavy, a masterpiece in itself. This is still a very active monastery and different families take it in turn to look after and officiate at the shrine. The people are very friendly and one of the boy monks will be pleased to take you up into the monastery to see the frescoes and other images of the Buddha. This is one of the few monastic buildings that is well endowed and where a conscious effort is made by its members to look after the building's structure and fabric.

South Patan: Mahabaudha and Machhendra

Returning to the main road, you can continue along it and take a sharp turning to the left, which will lead you back to the Durbar Square.

Having passed through the Durbar Square, take a turning left, in an easterly direction, through the vegetable market, and pass along a brick-paved street between terraced houses of a much later period. After several hundred metres (yards) the road opens out into a fairly large terrace square containing two stone *shikhara* temples and a water conduit. The water conduit is known as **Sundhara**, or golden tap, because of its beautiful gilded water-spouts. The exact history of this watering place is not certain but records show that it underwent renovation in 1701. This square is one of the important stopping places during the Rato Machhendranath Jatra festival (see page 171) and legend has it that the water-spouts were constructed to provide refreshment for the god.

At this point you take a right turn up a paved street. Almost at the top of the street there is a narrow entrance to the right which leads through to the rather special terracotta temple known as **Mahabaudha**. This *shikhara*-style temple is located in a narrow, irregular courtyard that must have been a monastery. Unfortunately, it is now dwarfed by ugly modern buildings. The design and material of the temple are unique in the Valley. All the façades are completely covered with hundreds of terracotta plaques in relief, each depicting the Buddha seated in a niche. The temple is built in two parts, a square base containing the shrine and a high tapering tower with four small pinnacles, one in each corner. This temple is said to be a copy of the Mahabodi Temple of Bodhgaya in Bihar, India. The builder, Abjayaraja Sakya, saw the original while on pilgrimage and, bringing back an image of the Buddha, decided to enshrine it in a similar structure. Apparently it took several generations to complete. During the violent earthquake of 1934, this temple was badly damaged. Subsequent efforts at repairing it were confounded by the very many parts that could not be put back during the renovation, and these were therefore assembled separately and now form a secondary shrine in one corner.

Turning right out of the alley, the main street takes a further sharp right turn. However, you are now looking for the **Uku Bahal** which is located off an opening to the left. This is one of the most famous Buddhist monasteries in Patan. It is probable that King Shivadeva had the temple built some time in the 1650s and performed his own initiation rites here. A very splendid doorway to the main shrine, with a decorative metal arch, was donated in 1676 and the struts supporting the first roof depicting the five Mahabuddhas were donated in 1653, all of which establishes this as one of the earlier *bahals*. The building is large and rectangular, with two tiers of roof. The upper roof is capped with a resplendent series of gilded pinnacles. The courtyard is filled with a wonderful collection of animals made of metal, as well as several important votive *chaityas*, which makes it a great favourite among visitors.

Returning to the main street, you continue straight ahead (along the route taken by the chariot) until you enter an area of **metalworkers** at a short distance from the main junction. In this *tol* you will see coppersmiths beating out brass and copper cooking pots of all sizes, from the domestic pot to enormous vessels used during festival picnics.

At the point where this road meets a main road, you turn left. A short way up the road there is an opening on both sides, leading on the right to the Machhendra Temple, and on the left to the **Min Nath**, which will be the first we visit. This is a small, two-tiered temple enshrining a Buddhist deity which is brought out during the great Machhendra festival and follows behind the big chariot dragged by local children. The temple has an elaborate entrance with latticed doors, a *torana*, and big prayer wheels. It was built by Halarchan Dev during the 16th century.

Across the road is the entrance to one of the most famous temples in Patan

The Craft of Repoussé Work

by Caroline Dyer

In the winding backstreets of Patan, you can discover artisans labouring over a craft that the rest of the world has almost forgotten: repoussé—the art of turning, chiselling and hammering a sheet of metal into a work of art.

Repoussé has been a feature of Nepali art since AD 607, when a repoussé cover for the most sacred Vaishnava cult image in Nepal, Changu Narayan, was fashioned. This piece is zealously guarded from the prying eyes of non-Hindus. The oldest example of Nepali repoussé which can be freely admired, however, is a plaque dating to AD 983 of the four-armed Vishnu, now reposing in the Los Angeles County Museum.

Many repoussé works were used to protect sacred stone images during prayer; others recorded land grants or similar donations. Free-standing icons, in carefully worked repoussé, were also common. By far the most ornate use of repoussé work was in the crowns worn by Buddhist masters. Inlaid with garnets, rubies, turquoise and other precious stones, with exquisitely worked figures on their sides, they were gilded with a dazzling layer of mercury amalgam.

You need go no further than the repoussé workers' home town of Patan to marvel at repoussé work. The Kwa Bahal temple here is covered with relief figures. But if you venture further afield, you will soon discover that repoussé works are as much a part of the whole Valley's landscape as the mountains themselves.

The time and care needed to produce exquisitely worked repoussé has meant that in many places the tradition has died out, but in Nepal it is still a vigorous part of daily life, and you may come across many recent examples of the craft. Bhaktapur's 18th-century repoussé gilt copper gate (see page 118) is a beautiful example of more modern craftsmanship, perfectly preserved and awe-inspiring in its attention to detail. Elsewhere, hidden away in many houses, are repoussé pots and vessels; many are very old, while others are perhaps fresh from the artisan's chisel or hammer.

Once in a while, repoussé works steal out of the background and are paraded in the streets of the Valley. During the Samek festival, held once every five years in Patan and, every 12 in Kathmandu, huge images of Dipankara Buddha, gilded and inlaid, are brought to Swayambhu where they are worshipped by upper-class Buddhist devotees. During the Indrajatra festival (see page 174), the ritual masks of Bhairab, often made of wood or metal but most impressive when chiselled from gilt copper, can be seen distributing alcohol through their mouths to jostling crowds.

Repoussé is as much a part of the present as it is a silent reminder of the past. And Nepal's masters are among the last in the world to practise their demanding craft, an unspoken tribute to a culture largely unaffected by the passage of time.

श्रीभीमसेनप्रीती ॥
सुवर्णकोमोलवाप
सं १९८९ साल आषाढस

and one of the most popular in the religious life of the community—the **Machhendranath** (the Machhendra Temple, or place of Machhendra), probably built by Shrinivasa Malla in the 1670s. It is a beautiful three-tiered structure located in a large, open park, with metal-covered roofs bordered with wind-bells. It has intricately carved doorways with flanking windows on each elevation. Each entrance is guarded by a pair of animals and the plinth is enclosed by a wall of prayer wheels. There are some very fine carved struts with representations of Avaloketeswar on the upper section, while beneath there are scenes of torture being meted out to condemned souls in hell. The deity represented in the shrine is Padmapani Avaloketeswar, popularly known as Machhendra. He is worshipped by all as the god of rain and plenty, hence the importance of the Machhendra festival just prior to the monsoon (see page 169). The god was originally the Bundyo of Bungamati, and each year the god spends three months in that town, an arrangement probably made by King Shrinivasa Malla.

Returning to the main road, you turn left out of the temple compound and walk down the hill, passing through the shops that sell metalwork. These are owned by the Tamrakar caste who beat and cast copper and brass articles for everyday use and for votive offerings in the temples.

One interesting little **shrine to Bishwakarma**, the god of the craftsmen, can be found down the alley on the left, shortly before you reach the Durbar Square. The shrine houses, in fact, an *agam* or private house god, worshipped by a *guthi* group. The façade of the shrine is of embossed and gilded copper, which was added in 1885. It is located at ground level in an open niche with a very decorative *torana* over it. Above the door is a window with an unusual solar disc and interlocking triangle design. Both the upper windows are flanked with interesting embossed images and divinities. The entrance is guarded by figures of Ganga and Yamuna.

To reach the Durbar Square, it will be necessary to retrace your tracks to the main road and continue northwards.

Bhaktapur

The Road to Bhaktapur

Bhaktapur, or Bhadgaon as it is sometimes called, is located in the eastern part of the Kathmandu Valley, about 19 kilometres (12 miles) from the centre of Kathmandu. The city is built along an east-west running ridge just above the Hanumante River, which defines the southern extremity of the city. When viewed from the Chinese Road, the city of Bhaktapur, as described in mythology, can be likened to a conch shell as it nestles into the surrounding countryside, the contours of the dwellings being broken occasionally by a towering temple structure. The backdrop is the ever-present snow peaks of the Himalaya which are often imitated by the swirling, billowing white clouds that may be covering them.

Access to Bhaktapur along the Kodari Highway, more commonly referred to as the Chinese Road, is made simple now with the Chinese trolley-bus service which runs between Tripureswar in Kathmandu to a depot to the south of Bhaktapur. Once at the Bhaktapur Depot, it is an easy and interesting walk across the Hanumante River and up the narrow roads which lead eventually into, first, the Taumadhi Tol and then the Durbar Square. By taxi it is best to negotiate a return trip for half a day to guarantee your homeward journey. By bicycle it is a small expedition, but it is worth dedicating a full day as there are many interesting places to stop for a moment en route. You may choose for instance to return on the old road through Thimi, which is famous for its terracotta pots and papier-mâché masks, or you may wish to wander through the paddy fields to watch the rice planting or harvesting —or prefer just to take a rest! About 12 kilometres (eight miles) from Kathmandu on the trolley-bus route you will pass the lower entrance to Thimi—the village is located on an escarpment overlooking the main road—where you will find an obvious turn-off to the left that leads towards the western end of Bhaktapur. The road bears right after crossing the Hanumante River and passes through a holy grove of pine trees. Look up into the higher branches of the trees: you may see colonies of fruit bats that spend the daylight hours at rest there.

The road passes through an army barracks, the fire station, which contains some interesting vintage fire engines, and past the notorious Siddhi Pokhari (see page 135). At this point the road divides and you can either take the lower, more traditional, route to the centre of Bhaktapur—best taken if you are on foot—or continue along the upper road which soon narrows and is enclosed by traditional brick-terraced dwellings. The road eventually opens into a space surrounded by a group of exquisite domestic buildings dating from the Malla period, which serve as a kind of threshold to the Durbar Square.

A Tour through the Bhaktapur Durbar Square

Unlike the other durbar squares, that of Bhaktapur is not in the city centre but lies to the north of the city and is linked only by small alleyways to the more important and imposing square known as the **Taumadhi Tol**, located southeast and below the Durbar Square.

The present Durbar Square is a shadow of its former self; much of it has disappeared as it was razed to the ground during the 1934 earthquake. It also suffered further damage in the 1988 earthquake. Legend has it that there were as many as 99 courtyards attached to this palace. In 1742, only 12 existed in reality, of which six remain today. The result of the earthquake is still evident; whereas in other areas temples were rebuilt, in this square the damage was so severe that, in many cases, only the bases remained. Prior to the earthquake, it seems there were three separate groups of temples in the square, but today it is empty, with buildings only on the fringes.

Access to many of the courtyards of the royal palace is not possible, except in the case of the Nag Pokhari and the areas you can see from the interesting museum building which is located in sections of the palace at first-floor level.

Let us first take a look at the palace buildings. It is difficult to determine exactly their early history, but it is believed they were built when the city was established in the ninth century. At that time, the palace was known as Tipura and was the seat of the *de facto* authority of the kingdom. None of the structures of this period remain and, generally, the information uncovered to date indicates that most of the palace, other than the Mul Chowk, dates from the late 16th and early 17th century.

Today, the focal point of the palace is the centrally placed **Golden Gate**, or **Sun Dhoka** as it is called. Facing this, the buildings to the left or west, which represent two wings of the palace, were constructed during the reign of Jagat Jyoti Malla (1613–37). They have since been much altered and today they form the major part of the museum.

The Sun Dhoka, often compared to Ghiberti's famous doors in the Baptistery in Florence, Italy, was erected in 1753 by Jaya Ranjit Malla, and is the finest example of gilded copperwork to be found in Bhaktapur and perhaps even in the Kathmandu Valley. It is very ornate and the panels around the doorframe, which depict a series of ten divinities including Ganesh, are in very fine repoussé work. The gate is capped with a small gilded roof surmounted with decorated finials and detailed images of winged lions and elephants. Although rather strangely located, the gate marks the entrance to the **Taleju Temple**.

One of the striking examples of Nepali artwork of the square is the **statue of King Bupatindra Malla** raised on a pillar opposite the Sun Dhoka. The king is kneeling on a throne supported by four lions which rest on a stone lotus flower. The king carries his weapons of war at his side but is in an

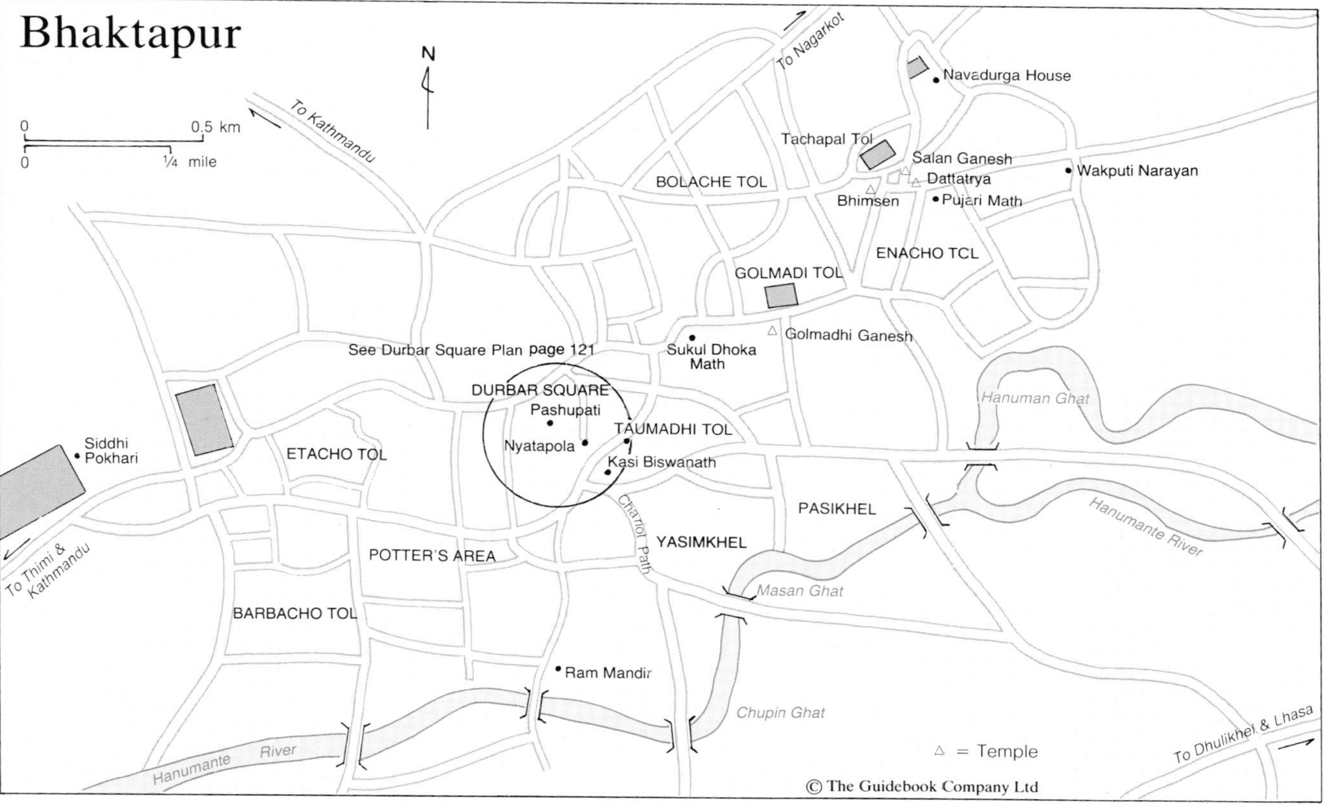
Bhaktapur
N
0 0.5 km
0 ¼ mile
To Kathmandu
To Nagarkot
Navadurga House
Tachapal Tol
Salan Ganesh
Dattatrya
Wakputi Narayan
BOLACHE TOL
Bhimsen
Pujari Math
ENACHO TCL
GOLMADI TOL
Golmadhi Ganesh
Sukul Dhoka Math
See Durbar Square Plan page 121
DURBAR SQUARE
Pashupati
TAUMADHI TOL
Nyatapola
Kasi Biswanath
Hanuman Ghat
Siddhi Pokhari
ETACHO TOL
PASIKHEL
Chariot Path
YASIMKHEL
Hanumante River
POTTER'S AREA
To Thimi & Kathmandu
Masan Ghat
BARBACHO TOL
Ram Mandir
Chupin Ghat
△ = Temple
To Dhulikhel & Lhasa
Hanumante River
© The Guidebook Company Ltd

attitude of prayer. He is dressed in the attire common in those days. This statue is a just tribute to a man who was responsible not only for renovating many of the buildings surrounding him but also for their construction.

Passing through the gate and a further low entrance door you enter what is known as **Beko Chowk**, which today appears to be the backs of a series of palace buildings and hardly the main route to reach Mul Chowk. Following this courtyard around to the left you will come to an entrance door with a carved wooden *torana* of exquisite beauty. Unfortunately, foreign visitors are not permitted beyond this doorway into the **Taleju Chowk** and the **Kumari Chowk**, which are said to contain some of the most important works of art in the Valley. The Kumari Chowk, which is attributed to Jitamitra Malla, is believed to be one of the gems of Nepali architecture. The foundation of the **Mul Chowk** dates back to the 13th century. Unlike the other two durbar squares, the Taleju shrine in Bhaktapur is not an impressively tall building, but a shrine of a single storey with rich ornamentation. By placing yourself judiciously in the doorway, it is possible to glimpse some of the beautiful gilded-copper images in front of the main shrine, the roof of which is capped with as many as 11 small spires and some rather exotic serpents that slide down the ribbed roof. This courtyard has been the subject of many donations by various Bhaktapur monarchs, but especially Bupatindra Malla.

In the northeast corner of the courtyard, a small wooden door leads into what was formerly a courtyard. Here there is a beautiful bathing pool known as **Nag Pokhari**. This bathing 'courtyard' was constructed in the early 17th century under the direction of Jagatir Malla, and later repaired by Jitamitra Malla when he had the wooden post with a gilded head of Vasuki, the snake god, erected. The sunken pool with its golden water-spout was formerly richly adorned with fine stone sculptures. It is probable that, as in the other durbar squares, it was originally surrounded by buildings. The water is said to be piped by conduit for seven miles. It is worth studying the remaining sculptures and in particular the gilded water-spout.

On your left as you re-enter the square there is an impressive wing of the palace built in 1697 by Bupatindra Malla and generally referred to as '**The Palace of the Fifty-five Windows**'. It is a buiding of three storeys with, on the lower storeys, finely carved windows and doors and, on the upper floor, an open hall with 55 arcaded windows. This upper floor formerly projected, but during the 1934 earthquake the building was badly damaged and had to be reconstructed.

Originally, on the right flank of the palace, there were further courtyards but all that remains of these today are the guardian lions. Similarly, several temples and resthouses succumbed in the earthquake and only a few base platforms remain. An interesting collection of different varieties and styles of temple remains nevertheless in the Durbar Square. At the entrance to the square is a two-tiered temple known locally as **Bansi Narayan**. It has the

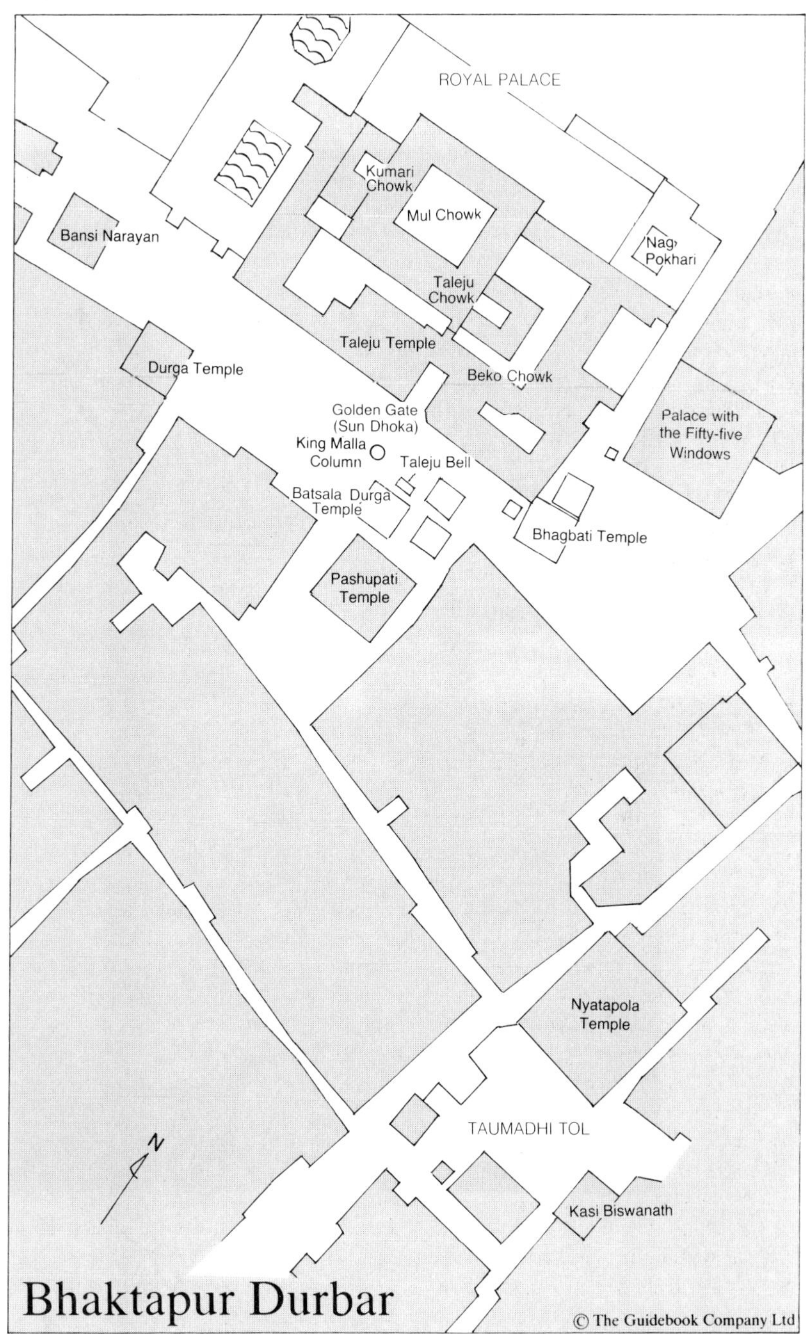

Bhaktapur Durbar

format of an early structure but its date of foundation is not known. The woodcarvings of the roof struts represent incarnations of Vishnu and the deity enshrined is Krishna.

Behind the Bansi Narayan is an interesting *shikhara*-style **temple to Durga**, the spouse of Shiva, built in a mixture of stone, brick, timber and terracotta. Commanding a focal position close to the Golden Gate is the impressive **temple of Batsala Durga**, one of two very beautiful stone *shikharas* in the Durbar Square. The construction of this temple, which is a close copy of the Krishna Temple in Patan, is attributed to Bupatindra Malla and was completed in the late 17th century. It underwent extensive repair at the hands of the Hanuman Dhoka Project Team. The temple boasts many stone carvings of various divinities. Other interesting features are the copper pinnacles and the wind-bells, which are an unusual feature on temples in the *shikhara* style. On the same platform as the Batsala Durga Temple are two bells: the large one, rung during the worship of Taleju, was erected by Ranajit Malla in 1737; the second, set adjacent to the entrance of the shrine, was placed there by Bupatindra Malla to counteract the ominous tone of a death knell which he had heard in a dream.

Adjacent to the Batsala Durga, on the northern side and close to the Palace with the Fifty-five Windows, is the **Bhagbati Temple**, the smaller of the two stone temples built in the *shikhara* style. It was erected in the 17th century, probably by Bupatindra Malla, and once again dedicated to Durga. Its most noteworthy features are the splendid pairs of guardians lining the steps to the sanctuary. In front of the sanctum, a series of relief panels depicts the Matrika goddesses.

The large two-tiered temple to the right of the Batsala Durga is known as the **Pashupati Temple**. This broad-based temple set on a low plinth was built by King Yaksha Malla, probably in the late 15th century, and has undergone several alterations during its history. It is said that Yaksha Malla was instructed by Lord Pashupati in a dream to build the temple. He was also told to visit the temple every day. On the one day he failed to appear, the Bagmati River flooded its banks. The temple does in fact resemble the main Pashupati Temple and there is also a small shrine to Gujeswari. The temple was severely damaged in the 1934 earthquake and most of it had to be rebuilt. The supporting roof struts are, however, from the original building and are of simple classical form, depicting Shiva and important characters from the *Ramayana*. Beneath, there are several examples of erotica.

Places to Discover in Bhaktapur

There are two worthwhile walks in Bhaktapur: one is beyond the Durbar Square to the Taumadhi Tol, containing the famous Nyatapola; the other is a tour through the eastern part of Bhaktapur, taking in the Tachapal Tol area where the famous Pujari Math and the Datatraya Temple are located.

The Taumadhi Tol is an extension of the Durbar Square, while the Tachapal area is a 20-minute walk through the streets of Bhaktapur. It is possible to drive there, but there are some interesting buildings and shrines to see on the way which you would otherwise miss.

Taumadhi Tol and Beyond

Following the narrow road beyond the Pashupatinath Temple you enter one of the most impressive squares, known as Taumadhi Tol, over which towers the **Nyatapola Temple**. This temple, built by Bupatindra Malla in 1702, is set on a stepped platform of five diminishing plinths and has five tiered roofs of beautifully tapering proportions. Despite its rather garishly painted exterior, the carvings to the arcaded pillars, windows and supporting roof struts are of exceptional beauty. The latter, numbering 108, are representations of the diverse forms of Bhagawati Mahishamardini and other lesser divinities. The eaves of all the roofs are edged with hundreds of small wind-bells. The **inner sanctum** contains a beautiful sculpture of Mahishamardini or Siddhi Lakshmi, but this shrine is only occasionally visited by select priests. The inner sanctum is approached up a long flight of steps which is lined with pairs of guardians in order of increasing power from the bottom. The lowest figures, standing about 2.5 metres (eight feet) high, represent Jai Mal and Patta, the famous wrestlers of Bhaktapur reputed to possess the strength of ten men. Above them stands a pair of elephants possessing ten times the strength of the wrestlers. Next come two lions ten times more powerful than the elephants. These are superseded by two griffons which outrank the strength of the lions by ten times. Finally, the stairway is topped by two minor deities, Simhini and Byhagrini, who both possess ten times the strength of the griffons. This ascendancy in strength implies that the multiplication of power culminates in the goddess here worshipped, who is dominant over all through her supreme though unseen strength.

It is said that, during the building of the temple, King Bupatindra Malla himself carried bricks to the site, inspiring the locals to carry in five days sufficient materials to build this enormous temple. An unusual feature of this temple is, it is said, that the sanctum containing the divinity is set within the plinth and not at the head of the steps as expected.

Close to the Nyatapola, on the eastern side of the square, is another important shrine with three roof tiers, the **Kasi Biswanath**, which is dedicated to Bhairab. It is said that the Nyatapola was built to counter the machinations of this impetuous Bhairab image. Its original construction as a single-storeyed building is attributed to Jagat Jyoti Malla, but in the early part of Bupatindra Malla's reign it was extended to its present form and completed in 1708. The present structure, however, was only reassembled after the 1934 earthquake, using parts of the original fabric. The temple is rectan-

gular, with the main shrine at ground level. There are three tiers of roofs, the uppermost being gilded sheet-metal surmounted with several ornate pinnacles. The supporting roof struts, of which there are 56, depict the forms of the Matrika and Bhagmati goddesses. During the festival of Bisket, an image of Bhairab is taken around in a chariot and he is identified with the image of Kasi Biswanath. According to legend, Biswanath came one day to see the Bisket festival in the disguise of a human being. A Tantric priest, recognizing him, wanted to capture him and started to bind him with *mantras*. Biswanath began to disappear but the priest, in despair, cut off his head, which is said to be enshrined in the temple.

This square, with its two main roads running diagonally across it, is of greater religious significance than the Durbar Square, as it is often used as a gathering place during the major festivals.

Taking the road in a westerly direction, it is worth looking at a very attractive group of traditional dwellings overlooking a small square located a short way along the road on the left-hand side. These houses belong to wealthy farmers and contain some very fine carved windows. The paved road and the excellent brickwork, which harmonizes well with the colour of the woodwork, help to make this a unique group of buildings. This road leads to the top end of the route that runs down to the river, and the one which the chariot has to negotiate during the Bisket festival (see page 170). Ignoring the rather unpleasant open drains, it is worth walking down the street which, at the bottom, opens out again into another beautiful streetscape. It is here, where the ground flattens out, that the main part of the Bisket festival takes place, when the image of Bhairab is removed from the chariot and placed in one of the small shrines and worshipped.

It is possible to cut through along one of the small paths to the right, at the point where the road opens out, but for the less intrepid it is wiser to return to the main road leading out of Taumadhi Tol and follow it to the left in a southerly direction. This road is most likely the former main trading and pilgrimage route through Bhaktapur. Follow it for about 100 metres (yards) and then, by turning left, you should arrive in the district where most of the potters of Bhaktapur live. The road opens out into a square which is usually filled with potters working at their wheels. It is hard to find a way through the hundreds of pots of all shapes and sizes that are drying in the sun prior to their baking in the kilns behind the square. Obviously, this trade is dependent on the weather and is mostly carried out when the craftsmen have time to spare from their agricultural work.

Returning again to the Taumadhi Tol, you can either retrace your tracks to the Durbar Square and drive to Tachapal or, if walking, cross the square on the diagonal and follow the road leading into the eastern sector of the town.

The Ramayana

by Kakoli Thompson

The Sanskrit epic, *Ramayana*, was originally a secular work recited at courts by bards. Like the *Mahabharata*, its central story was composed in the fifth or fourth century BC, and it continued to gather material for several centuries afterwards.

The *Ramayana* gained religious significance when its central figure, Rama, came to be identified as an incarnation of the Lord Vishnu, the supreme being. Even from the beginning, important issues of conduct were central to the plot, so Rama's deification can be understood to be the result of the portrayal of his character.

Ravana, the most dangerous and powerful demon king that ever lived, rules over Lanka (today's Sri Lanka). By practising austerities he has managed to propitiate Brahma, the creator in the Hindu trinity, who grants him immunity from being killed at the hands of gods, celestial spirits, or demons.

In return the gods consult with each other to see how they can be rid of Ravana; they hit on a god who would take human form, for Ravana had been too proud to ask for immunity from mortals.

Vishnu agrees to be the one and is born to the wives of a King Dasaratha, who had performed a great sacrifice in order to have heirs. Dasaratha is thus blessed with four sons: Ramachandra (Rama), the oldest, who has half of Vishnu's nature, Bharatha, who has a quarter, and Lakshmana and Satrughna, who have an eighth each. Rama and Lakshmana are particularly close.

Vishnu's wife, Lakshmi, has taken human form as the beautiful Princess Sita, daughter of King Janaka. In a contest for Sita's hand, her suitors have to bend a mighty bow given to her father by the Lord Shiva, the destroyer in the Hindu trinity. Rama not only succeeds, but actually breaks the bow!

Soon after Rama's marriage to Sita, Dasaratha abdicates, passing the throne to Rama. Everything seems perfect for the young couple, but evil forces are at work.

A malicious servant of Queen Kaikeyi, Bharatha's mother, incites her mistress to plot against Rama. The queen begs a favour from her husband who kindheartedly consents without asking what it is. When King Dasaratha learns that he has agreed to Baratha's succession to the throne instead of Rama, and that Rama is to be banished to the forest for 14 years, he dies of grief within a week.

So it is that Rama, his loving wife Sita, and his dear brother Lakshmana leave the court. Bharatha, who has been away during all this, is furious with his mother on his return, and blames her for his father's death. He goes to the forest to beg Rama to return to Ayodhya, the capital, and take his rightful place on the throne.

But Rama insists that he is honour-bound to remain in exile. Baratha returns, dejected, and reigns as viceroy, keeping a pair of Rama's slippers on the throne to symbolize his kingship.

In the forest, Rama and Lakshmana spurn the amorous advances of Ravana's sister, the giantess Surpanakha, and thus incur her wrath. Surpanakha attacks Sita, but Lakshmana in turn attacks the giantess, cutting off her nose, ears and breasts.

After a futile attempt at vengeance, Surpanakha turns to her brother, Ravana, and tells him of Sita's incredible beauty. She convinces him that Sita would make him a fitting wife. Ravana devises a clever plan and succeeds in carrying Sita off to Lanka in his aerial chariot.

On the way, Jatayu, an incarnation of Garuda, Vishnu's mount, and king of vultures, cries to stop Ravana but is fatally wounded, living just long enough to return to the forest and tell Rama what has happened.

Rama gathers forces against Ravana, taking as his main ally Hanuman, the monkey king of divine parentage whose supernatural powers and superb fighting skills prove invaluable in the fight for Rama's cause.

In Lanka, Sita rejects all Ravana's advances, and her abduction leads inexorably to the climax of the whole poem, the siege of Lanka and Ravana's eventual defeat. This represents a conflict between good and evil, while the long search for Sita amply demonstrates Rama's devotion to his wife.

The epic originally ended in a joyful reunion followed by a triumphant return to Ayodhya, the 14 years of exile having conveniently expired. In a reworking, the text now extant has Rama recognized as divine by a contingent of the gods, led by Brahma, while Sita has to undergo an ordeal by fire to prove her chastity before Rama will accept her back.

Taumadhi to Tachapal

After turning slightly to the right, the route leads through an area crowded with shops. On the right, set into the line of shops, you will come across an impressive building which has recently undergone renovation. The building, known as the **Sukul Dhoka Math**, was built by Ranajit Malla in about 1740 for a group known as the Sanyasis of Lakshmanapuri, and an endowment was set up by the king for daily worship to take place. In 1744, the king placed a Banalingeswari *lingam* in the shrine.

Here the woodcarvings are of exceptional quality, especially the windows on the first floor. The future of this building was only recently assured, as its condition before renovation was very dilapidated. During its repair, the main façade was consolidated, the former shop-openings were filled in and the building was returned to its original form. The courtyard behind was gutted and rebuilt, and the renovated building will now be put to a more suitable use.

Continuing along the road, on the right is a small three-tiered temple, known as **Golmadhi Ganesh**, built in the mid-17th century. Opposite there is a large and deep *hiti*, or tank, that has recently undergone repair. There are several interesting stone sculptures, some of them quite early, set in niches around the spout.

Beyond, the road widens, and in the shops on the right dyers can be found hand-printing and dyeing the traditional local cloth. The road climbs a slight incline and from here on the work of the Bhaktapur Development Project will become evident. The streets have been repaved, the plinths of the houses reformed and storm-water and sewage drains have been introduced. This street eventually opens out on to the focal point of this project, the area known as **Tachapal Tol**. Here, all the important buildings have undergone restoration, water tanks have been cleaned out and repaired and a sewage system has been installed as well as a new drinking-water supply.

Tachapal Tol and Beyond

Surrounding the square there are several *maths*, the most important being the **Pujari Maths**, several small temples and shrines, and a fair number of important private dwellings. Dominating the square at the eastern end is the famous **Dattatrya Temple**, one of the most renowned not only of Bhaktapur but of the whole Valley. It was originally built as a *mandapa* and its similarity to the Kasthamandapa in Kathmandu is fairly evident. It is much smaller but nonetheless impressive. It only became known as Dattatrya Temple because the front part of the building was added later to house the images of Shiva, Brahma and Dattatraya. A stone inscription states that a small shrine was built to commemorate the spot where a famous guru died. This shrine was later enlarged by Yaksha Malla in about 1427 as a *chapara*, a type of pilgrims' resthouse. During the reign of Viswa Malla, the building was

extended to form the temple as it stands today to serve as both a place of rest and an important shrine. The images in the temple represent the three major gods of the Hindu trinity. The entrance is protected again by the famous wrestlers of Bhaktapur, Jai Mal and Patta, who are flanked by the symbols of the deities within. Beyond, there is a fine image of Garuda set on a high pillar.

Just behind and slightly to the right is a building closely associated with the Dattatraya Temple—the **Pujari Math**, one of the most important *math* to be found in the Valley. In this square alone, there are nine different *maths*; as only 30 *maths* have been identified in the whole Valley, the importance of this square can be appreciated.

The construction date of the Pujari Math is uncertain and steeped in legend. However, there are records stating that a *math* was built on this site during the reign of King Yaksha Prakash Malla (1428–82); records show that it was consecrated and opened for public *puja* during the year 1480. During Raja Viswa Malla's reign, it is also recorded that intensive renovations were carried out to restore the building to its original form. Later, in 1763, further extensions and alterations were made by the *mahanta*, or chief priest of the time. The *math* suffered considerable damage during the 1934 earthquake, and it was with German aid that the building once again underwent major repair with a view to restoring it to its original condition. Today, the *math* has been converted into an important local museum and is open to visitors.

Although rather imposing, the exterior of the Pujari *math* has fairly standard styles of carving, except for some windows down a side alley which are carved in the form of a strutting peacock, a symbol which today gives the monastery its more common references. However, the exterior of the building belies the true brilliance of the carvings in the inner courtyard which surpass nearly all other examples of carving so far discussed with the exception of that found in the Hanuman Dhoka Palace. The courtyard was probably the result of the 18th-century renovations and is worth close study. There is a profusion of details in the windows, cornices and pillars, all of which are of highly complicated design. The brickwork is also unusual. It is much darker and the joints are sealed with a resinous mixture known as *saldup*, a system apparently used only in Bhaktapur.

You will find a considerable amount of information available about the development programme as there is a permanent exhibition mounted in one of the rooms in the Pujari Math. Some of the upper rooms are painted with interesting murals, an unusual feature in Nepali buildings and, should they be accessible, they are well worth visiting.

Returning once again to the bottom end of the square, there is an interesting two-storey building dedicated to Bhimsen. It was constructed in 1605 and contains an unusual earthen image of Bhimsen. The lower floor is designed as a *pathi* with a small door looking out over the newly restored series of water conduits behind. Over the main shrine there is a gilded roof capped by several unusual pinnacles. It is worth taking a closer look at some of the façades of the other nine Bhaktapur *maths* overlooking the square.

Returning to the top of the square and continuing along the narrow road beside the Dattatraya, you will pass several other recently renovated buildings. Towards the end of the road, on the right, there is a small but delightful temple complex. This temple, known as **Wakupati Narayan**, is dedicated to Garud Narayan and, although probably of early construction, its exact date is not known. The small two-tiered temple set in a neat stone-paved courtyard is extensively covered or decorated with metal. The doorway is of embossed metal and the *torana*, the roof and the finials are all of gilded copper. Take a close look at the details on the roof: the small sun heads at the rib ends, the birds sitting on the corner pieces, and the highly ornate pinnacle with the inscribed metal ribbon falling down the roof from it. In front of the temple are several fine metal symbols and two beautiful *garudas*.

Wakupati Narayan is almost at the easternmost extreme of Bhaktapur. Continuing a short way beyond the complex, take a sharp left turn up a hill through a residential area. At almost the top of this road, you will arrive outside a simple building following almost the style and proportions of the dwellings you have just passed. This is in fact what is known as an *agam* house, in which a god belonging to a particular sect is kept. This one is the dwelling of Navadurga and her associates, who are important for their roles in the religious lives of the people of Bhaktapur. A troupe of masked dancers, known as the Navadurga, perform ritual dances at all the major festivals in Bhaktapur throughout the year. The dancers, who come from a class known as Banamala, are highly venerated and greatly feared. The masks for this dance are kept on the first floor of this building, a dark, sinister place smelling of blood from the many sacrifices associated with the Tantric rites performed to appease the goddess and her associates. The final dance at the end of July enacts the ritual death of Navadurga. During the dance, the masks are smashed and burnt. The goddesses are reborn once more during Dasain, with the creation and dedication of new masks which will survive the year. These masks are made in papier-mâché by local craftsmen.

The building itself is typical of the *agam*-house style. It is a long rectangular structure with two storeys and a single pitched roof. The windows and doors have ornately carved *toranas* and the supporting roof struts depict the ten matrika.

At the end of the road there is a large tank surrounded by further dwellings. Turning left alongside the tank, walk to the end of this open space and turn left again to follow a narrow alley that leads you back into the Tachapal Tol. You will pass a small temple known as **Salan Ganesh**, dedicated to the Ganesh that is strongly linked with the Taleju shrine in the palace.

From Tachapal Tol, retrace your tracks to the Durbar Square.

On your return to Kathmandu, it is worth while stopping briefly to take a look at the **Siddhi Pokhari**, an enormous tank located close to the army headquarters in Bhaktapur. It is on built-up ground near the Tundikhel and measures nearly 100 metres (yards) long. The tank was constructed in the 16th century and legend has it that a serpent of untold size lives in the waters. For fear that it may emerge, the tank is never emptied. Even now the inhabitants of Kirtipur do not dare enter the compound! Several additions have been made to the tank throughout its history, the most recent by King Mahendra in 1958.

If you have time to spare, it is worth returning to Kathmandu along the old route passing through **Thimi**, a place that is famous for its pottery. On the road just outside the town there is a small shop where renowned papier-mâché masks are made.

If you are in Nepal during the dry season you will see the brickyards out in the fields along the roadside where the Nepalis have been making their bricks for centuries. It is in these fields that the first of the new batch of the special glazed bricks was made and the regeneration of an old craft began (see pages 60–2).

Other Sights around the Kathmandu Valley

The Banepa Valley

Beyond the city of Bhaktapur, about five kilometres (three miles) to the east, the road wends its way through a series of agricultural amphitheatres of terraced rice fields that are an everchanging quilt of colour. The road follows the original trail from the Kathmandu Valley proper into the adjacent lush Banepa Valley en route for Tibet. Because of its abundance of significant artefacts, the Banepa Valley is always considered culturally to be part of the Kathmandu Valley although topographically it belongs to another watershed.

Banepa—a Small Trading Centre

Legend has it that Ananda Malla, who founded Bhaktapur, created seven major settlements on the eastern side of the Valley in order to strengthen his new kingdom. On the edge of the Valley, the small settlement of Sanga defines the watershed between the two valleys and the transition is usually very marked as the Banepa Valley, clearly defined by the surrounding hills and of a slightly higher altitude, is in a later period of cultivation, contrasting greatly to the terraces above Bhaktapur. It is also extremely fertile. You are brought back to harsh reality on approaching the fast-developing trading centre of Banepa, which demonstrates all the hideous aspects of uncontrolled ribbon development along the highway. It has encouraged the strangest forms of construction and, as a staging post for public transportation, the town has the typical attributes of a characterless Terai truck stop. However, hidden in the town and behind it are the products of a former Newari culture that is struggling to survive. By turning left in a northerly direction along the main street you will get swept up in the bustle of a typical trading post which supplies the surrounding villages—taking over from the earlier crossroads at Panauti. In the heart of the town, on a slightly raised site to the left, is a pair of **temples to Vishnu**. These temples have been recently renovated by a team trained at the Hanuman Dhoka. The temples have some exquisite carvings, which at the time of conservation were free of polychrome.

Chandeswari—an Unspoilt Hamlet

Returning along the main street, almost to the entry point of the town, you will locate a pond at a crossroads with a road leading to the east, or left. This trail, formerly paved with stone flags, leads to Chandeswari and on to Helambu in the upper foothills of the Himalaya. This was the route that all major expeditions to Everest used to take. The road passes a small Seventh Day Adventist cottage hospital—now the most important medical facility in this area—through gently undulating paddy fields into the almost unspoilt hamlet of Chandeswari. As you reach the edge of the settlement, the trail will be lined with cattle, drying grain and all the activities associated with a small farming community. The road comes to an abrupt end in front of the entrance to the **temple of Chandeswari**. Here a tribute to religious fervour manifests itself in concrete modernism—an intricately carved entrance painstakingly translates the beauty and excellence of traditional woodcarving to a stucco concrete. Inside this compound is a beautiful three-tiered temple with an exceptional **mural of Bhairab** on the western wall. Legend has it that the Valley was at one time full of wild beasts considered by the locals to be demons. They called upon Parvati to rid them of Chand, a demon they greatly feared. Once rid of this beast, the deity became known as Chandeswari, the slayer of Chand and, in gratitude, the locals built this magnificent temple.

The compound, located on the edge of a holy forest, overlooks a small stream that leads to an interesting collection of *ghats* below. The temple is set in a wide precinct, now being modernized for pilgrims, but there is an unusual assembly of metal animals set on pillars in front of the temple. The temple itself, dating from the 17th century, is a powerful structure with an inner sanctum housing the image of Chandeswari which is bedecked in silver ornaments. The temple, which was wrecked by the 1934 earthquake, is a massive timber-framed structure which has been altered through the centuries. Perhaps the most striking memory of the temple will be the enormous colourfully painted image of Bhairab.

Once a year, in August, Chandeswari is taken on a bucolic chariot procession to Banepa and back. It is a bizarre sight to see this procession silhouetted against the dawn sky, the palanquin bearers staggering under their precious load—a truly mediaeval vignette.

Panauti—at the Confluence of Two Rivers

Retrace your steps to the turn-off point in Banepa and continue across the main road in a westerly direction towards Panauti. The road crosses a bridge and then wends its way through a beautiful agrarian landscape alongside the river. There is plenty happening along the route as you pass through small hamlets. Round a bend you will be confronted with a slab of new construction heralding your arrival in Panauti—once a thriving traditional trading post. Today this unique little town, formerly unspoilt by development, has tried to retain its importance by re-establishing its trading potential over the more accessible Banepa. However, once through the modern outskirts, follow the main route above the Roshi Khola River past a couple of derelict *pathis*. Before you enter the first open space, there is a fine example of a *sattal* on the left, close to a group of sunken stone water-spouts. The large open space beyond was formerly the site of a large Taleju temple and palace complex. All that remains today is a small brick *shikhara* and a grassy mound. Continue down the main street, passing traditional terraced dwellings, towards the religious heart of the town.

Panauti is built on the confluence of two rivers, which makes it a very holy site. The stunning temple complex, dominated by the **Indreswar Mahadev**, is located at the point of the confluence. The towering Indreswar temple is reputedly one of the oldest standing structures in the Kathmandu Valley. Dating from the early 15th century, the temple exhibits the simple classical form of the early style. The strong but uncluttered designs of the doorways, the simple but sensuous carved images of Shiva on the roof struts, unmatched elsewhere in the Valley, and the powerfully proportioned diminishing roofs, make this one of the most rewarding places to visit in Nepal.

At the confluence are a further collection of temples of mixed design and the burning *ghats*. It is here that the peaceful Roshi Khola and the roaring Punyamati Khola meet and flow on, bearing the spirits, both good and bad, from Panauti. Isolated on the northern banks of the Roshi is a beautiful **temple to Bramayani**. This structure, which had become almost a ruin, has been painstakingly restored by a team from the Hanuman Dhoka Project. A non-existent foundation had to be replaced with a great deal of cunning so as not to disturb the wrath of the goddess housed in the temple.

To complete an unusual day of adventure, return to the now familiar statue of His Late Majesty King Mahendra atop his pedestal in Banepa and turn right (north) along the main road towards the Chinese border which passes through Dulikhel—one of the main viewing points on the edge of the Valley. Remember the intimacy of the villages you have just passed as you cross the rim of the Valley and see the expanse of foothills, terraces and, hopefully, if the sky is clear, mountains that spread beyond you. Spend the night at on e of the many lodge resorts from where, in the casual comfort of Nepali hospitality, the setting and rising of the sun on the mighty Himalaya is an experience that you will never forget.

The Gokarna Mahadev—a Unique Temple Complex

About 15 kilometres (ten miles) to the northeast of the city of Kathmandu, beyond the famous Buddhist shrine of Bauddha, lies the small village settlement of Gokarna on the northwestern corner of the King's Forest. At this point the most sacred river in the Valley, the Bagmati, passes from its torrential stage through a dark and mysterious gorge and into the fertile paddy fields of the Valley. At this sacred spot, along the western banks of the river, the holy Hindu complex of **Gokarna Mahadev** was founded in the 14th century and still lies almost unchanged as one of the most important temples of the Kathmandu Valley.

Approaching the temple compound from the south along the small dirt road leading from Baudhanath, the three-tiered temple of Mahadev, built in the traditional Newari style and dedicated to Shiva, appears above a collage of domestic structures of brick, mud and stone as a statement of religious fervour. The compound is set slightly below the approach road, nestling into the early stages of the gorge, with steps to the main entrance to the east of the temple rising directly from the river bed.

The founding of this religious site goes back many centuries to long before the present temple, or indeed Hinduism, controlled it. Every year, there is an important Buddhist festival when thousands of devout Newari Buddhists of the Kathmandu Valley flock to the river banks to commemorate their dead. There is also a diversity in the scope of Hindu worship as the main divinity belongs to Shiva's pantheon, whereas a small prayer hall, the **Vishnu Paduka**, where Hindus from the Valley and surrounding hills perform their after-death ceremonies is, as its name implies, dedicated to Vishnu. Similar to the Buddhist ceremony, on a day in mid-August known as the Gokarna Aunshi or Father's Day, families who are mourning the loss of a male member of their family visit Gokarna to pray for the departed soul and afterwards enjoy a family picnic at which time living fathers are also honoured (see page 173).

Over the centuries and especially the last few decades, this compound has been diminished by the exigencies of the river, the weather and the 1934 earthquake. In its prime, it consisted of not only the main temple, the Vishnu Paduka prayer hall, and a small shrine housing Parvati, but also of two priest houses—one for each of the caretaker priests of the main shrines—a small *bhajan pathi* or resthouse where religious songs were sung, a large resthouse for pilgrims, and a host of small votive shrines at the back of the complex.

The Mahadev Temple is typical of the traditional temple style of the 14th–16th centuries. It has a three-tiered timber roof structure built off solid brick walls enclosing a timber frame. The roof structure, which is covered with traditional tiles, is supported by carved *tunasi* or roof struts. Below the lowest roof, at ground level, the openings into the sanctum are decorated with very fine woodcarvings depicting divinities, worshippers, animals and floral patterns in great detail and reflecting the lifestyle of the people of that time. Access to the sanctum is through a gilded-metal inner doorway of exquisite proportions and detail which is seldom seen by the public. As well as the common structural failures found in this type of building, the woodcarvings were badly disfigured by an annual coating of mustard oil, intended formerly as a spiritual cleansing as well as a protection for the timber. However, latterly this practice had been maintained using old engine oils, with the result that the carvings were totally masked with a 12 millimetre (half-inch)-thick glutinous coating of congealed oils.

The Vishnu Paduka had lost its original roof, probably during the 1934 earthquake. It was later replaced by a corrugated-metal-sheet roof which leaked badly and offered little protection to the timber roof structure below. It is a wonder how the structure managed to stand, as fungal and beetle attack to the timbers had caused almost total structural collapse. Added to this, the foundations, disturbed by the rise and fall of the river, had settled considerably. During a heavy monsoon when the river is in spate, the flood rushes for a few hours through the prayer hall to a depth of almost two metres (six feet) above floor level.

Of the two priests' dwellings, one had been abandoned as its collapse was imminent, and the other was considered uninhabitable because its roof was leaking and part of one wall was sliding into the gorge. These have now been conserved and rehabilitated as part of the conservation project.

Originally the compound was closed on the south side by a *pathi* for pilgrims. The compound itself is paved in stone with bastion-like stone steps leading down to the river. Decades ago a zealous patron of the Mahadev temple made an important collection of stone sculptures of some rare and fine images which he donated to the temple. Beyond the compound, to the south, is an assorted collection of plastered brick votive shrines, mostly of a later period, housing many Shiva *linga*. Sadly, these have been totally neglected and most have fallen prey to the destructive pipal tree, whose roots have torn the structures asunder into a state of total ruin.

The Conservation Project

The Gokarna Conservation Project came about in response to the UNESCO international campaign. The project was supported from funds donated by the World Monuments Fund, based in New York. It represents, in many ways, the fulfilment of the objective of the Government of Nepal and UNESCO's joint undertaking in the Hanuman Dhoka Conservation Project. At Gokarna, the students of the Hanuman Dhoka Project were put to the test. Experienced working foremen in each of the key crafts were sent with a limited team of trained craftsmen to undertake the repair of the main temple under the control of staff from the Department of Archaeology, and the work proceeded following the Hanuman Dhoka 'pattern book'. The project had all the varying elements and problems necessary to make it a challenge to the team, without being too complicated or fraught with difficult structural problems. In fact, the structure of the main temple was very sound and the majority of the work lay in the refurbishing of the roof, using and adapting techniques well established at Hanuman Dhoka, and the daunting task of cleaning and conserving the woodcarvings.

Several of the large timber rafters on the roofs had to be replaced with new ones and the structure was consolidated with the dexterous placement of hand-forged metal ties and plates. The skills of the woodcarvers were tested in the replacement of one of the large roof struts or *tunasi*. The vegetation, which roots in the clay bed under the tiles during the monsoon, was brought under control by mixing a powerful herbicide with the clay. The tiles were treated with a very dilute silicone compound to prevent them from absorbing moisture, doubling their weight and becoming themselves a good seed bed.

The removal of the oil coating on the woodcarvings was not a simple matter, nor had a remedy been found previously. It was only the dogged determination of one of the Conservation Laboratory technicians that provided a simple yet effective method of removing the coating.

For a technique to be practicable, it is essential that all the materials should be available in Nepal and the method of application simple. Nothing could have been simpler than the one adopted. Clay was dug from the river bed and mixed into a paste using concentrated ammonia. The paste was applied as a poultice over the carvings and left for several hours to soften the oil coating. The poultice was then removed, bringing much of the coating with it. In its softened state it was possible to scrape off more of the deposit and the process was repeated until the carvings were exposed in their natural state. A team of 16 local girls was trained to undertake this time-consuming work. On average, one person was able to clean an area of about 30 by 30 centimetres (one square foot) in two days and it took a painstaking 18 months to clean all four façades. A small section on the northern door has been left uncleaned for comparison.

The second stage of the programme concentrated on the Vishnu Paduka. The foundations to the main pillars as well as to the perimeter pillars were non-existent. If a new tiled roof was to replace the present corrugated sheets, a very considerable load would be added to the already frail structure. It was decided to dismantle the whole building, after preparing a set of drawings and referencing each piece of carving and structure. The timber structure was dismantled and partly reassembled at ground level to enable new structural timbers to be fitted into the roof frame. While this work was in progress, investigations were carried out on the foundations, and archaeological explorations unearthed the original ritual offerings placed beneath the building—a small copper pot with the *panch ratna* or five precious stones, and a collection of coins in it.

The priests were insistent that a rededication was necessary and weeks went by awaiting the auspicious moment to reconsecrate the foundations. When the time came, on an early fog-shrouded morning, the team assembled at the site to witness a very colourful ceremony. A foundation stone was consecrated by washing it with milk and water from the seven holy seas (rivers, in reality), blessed with holy oils and daubed with honey and coloured powder before it was escorted to the bottom of the three-metre (ten-foot) -deep foundation pit. A new *kailash* or copper pot was placed beneath the stone with the old jewels and coins; gold, silver, and some present-day coins were added to commemorate the renovation.

At the top of the foundation plinth a new foundation grid was added to distribute the point loads from the columns evenly over the whole plinth. Slowly, the timber structure was rebuilt reusing, wherever possible, the old timbers. The roof was relaid, using the traditional *jhingati* tiles, and the old

Close Encounters of a Different Kind

My first visits to the Gokarna Mahadev complex were marked by strange encounters. A team from the Department of Archaeology of the Nepal Government accompanied me to plan the conservation project. We first visited the site on a cold, bright morning in January 1980 to discuss problems related to the repair and conservation of the temple as well as to meet the local village dignitaries and obtain their consent. As this was the first religious building our team had undertaken there was concern as to whether foreigners would be tolerated. We met the local village representatives who were cautious about foreign involvement but finally accepted our help.

However, we were soon to find out where the opposition lay as we were confronted with a strange, wild-looking *sadhu* or holy man, scantily dressed in orange robes, with a tall top-knot of unkempt hair and a hostile look in his eyes. He had taken up residence, uninvited, in one of the resthouses and was controlling the site. Apparently dumb, his cryptic comments were written in chalk on a child's slate and these were periodically thrust under the noses of the Nepali team. They replied in a similar manner. It seems the *sadhu* had taken exception to the presence of an 'Amrikan' and was threatening me with his literary talent. Liberal translations of his obscure messages interrupted our discussions, much to the amusement of all present, but it was very clear he strongly resented my interference even after I had professed my British nationality. I undertook subsequent visits with some fear and trepidation as, during our next encounter, the *sadhu* had laid down his slate and taken up his *trisul* or trident, a lethal metal weapon, with which he proceeded to chase me around the temple—a source of great amusement to the local children. The *sadhu* was later to attack, with an axe, the team photographer who fortunately managed to defend himself with his heavy tripod!

Subsequently, the *sadhu* was forcibly removed by the law, but he was later to appear at the project, having regained his speech. He told my chief carpenter on the site that he had made a vow of silence for 14 years because of the injustices in the world. From then on, my arrivals on the scaffolding at site were heralded by the boom of the conch shell which he would blow whilst circumambulating the temple—an equally unnerving experience.

carved doors, windows and grilles were cleaned and repaired.

Although somewhat off the beaten track, the Gokarna Mahadev compound is a favourite spot for the discerning traveller. Over the years of renovation, there has been a constant flow of visitors wishing to see and learn about the building conservation activities. The achievements of the craftsmen and the project administrators are certainly a credit to both their dedication and enthusiasm, and a just reward for all the efforts that have gone into the whole Conservation Movement in Nepal. It is also an apt answer to the question one is so often asked, 'Are there any craftsmen left in the Kathmandu Valley?'

Changu Narayan—An Early Hindu Settlement

Changu Narayan is one of the earliest religious settlements of the Kathmandu Valley—a Hindu site similar to the Buddhist one of Swayambhu. Set on a rock 'peninsula' running from the Nagarkot range to the east, Changu would have been prominent when the Valley was a lake. If you reach there early in the morning, the low-lying mist will create this illusion for you.

For those in a hurry to reach this unique and holy site, the quickest way is to drive up the recently developed road from behind Bhaktapur. Follow the road to Nagarkot, well known to any taxi driver. After about five kilometres (three miles), turn left between two *pathis* and continue along the single-file track that wends its way through a beautiful agrarian landscape and climbs rather precariously up the side of the hill on which the site is located.

However, the best way to reach Changu is to walk there following one of the routes described below. Either way, you will enter the village from the south and wander up the old stone-paved road past crumbling resthouses and a beautiful stone fountain on your right. Scattered about this complex are some fine old sculptures which today are used as somewhere to dry laundry! After a ten-minute climb, you will reach the main entrance to the temple. On the right you pass some interesting stone statues of Draupadi and Jaya, part of the unique collection of Licchavi sculptures of this site. The temple is surrounded on all sides by a two-storeyed structure where pilgrims used to stay during major festivals. The building delineates and protects the sublime and peaceful courtyard in which the main temple and a profusion of unique and exquisite sculptures reside.

The **Temple of Changu Narayan** is one of the most celebrated Vaishnava shrines of the Valley and its origin dates back to at least the fourth century but probably earlier. The earliest stone inscriptions in the Valley, dating from AD 500, are found on the stone columns at the entrance to the main shrine. Of course the present structure is of a much later date, having been erected in the first decade of the 18th century, reusing much of the decorative fabric. Between the first and present structure it is likely that there have been several reconstructions following fires and earthquakes. Nonetheless, the existing temple is a well-proportioned two-tiered temple, with a gilded-copper upper roof. The lower tiled roof is supported off some finely carved roof struts depicting the Dashavatar of Vishnu. The extra braces are not original but were placed there as additional support to the heavy roof. Colour was also added, following a trend that had become popular in the Valley in the 1950s. The main entrance to the shrine, guarded by two fearsome lions, is through an exquisite gilded triple doorway crowned by a *torana* depicting Narayan.

Facing the entrance are the fifth-century Vaintej or human-faced Garuda, a slight enigma to historians, and enclosed in a gilded cage are the beautiful 17th-century statues of Bupatindra Malla and his queen, the temple's benefactors.

road to the right into the campus and bear left towards the small city. Not so long ago the settlement crowned the tops of the hillocks and was divided from its fertile paddy fields by the steep hillsides. Today the University has acquired most of the farmland, and an unattractive urban sprawl known as Naya Bazaar has spilled around the base of the hill.

Kirtipur is still essentially a pedestrian city with narrow brick- and stone-paved roads running the length of the city along the contours of the hillock, with small paths making up a grid of access routes.

Formerly, the people of Kirtipur were either farmers (Jyapus) or merchants from the Shrestha clan. Land acquisition by the University has changed the character of Kirtipur and people have been forced to seek work in the city. However, the traditional craft of weaving is making a comeback and your tour through the city will be accompanied by the rhythmic 'clack-clack' of the looms.

Time has apparently stood still in upper Kirtipur. As you wander in search of the few important sites, you will notice that many fine domestic façades remain intact and some of the most distinguished and complete terraces still survive. One interesting and unusual feature you will see is that, due to the topography of the hills, the houses are narrow and the front access to them is at upper-floor level, so you can look from the houses to see either the trees and gardens beyond or across to the Valley below.

One of the direct approaches to Kirtipur from the west is up a long flight of steps towards a large pond. If you reach the plateau by car, turn left at the top of the hill and you will arrive at the same pond. Pass the large pipal tree which cradles a beautiful Lokeswar shrine and make towards the **Chilanchu Stupa** on raised ground a short distance from the pipal tree. Chilanchu is an ancient Buddhist *stupa* surrounded by four similar but smaller shrines, all following the style of Swayambhu, with stone images set at the cardinal points. This group was founded in the early 16th century. Close by, on the western edge of the compound, you will find the **Jagat Pal Vihara** which was built by the founder of the complex, Mahapatra Jagatpal Varma, in 1514. If you are lucky you may locate the small *bahals* of Chve and Kwe which are hidden behind simple traditional domestic facades.

Pass through the open space of Chilanchu to the north and continue in a northwesterly direction. You will soon find yourself, having passed down a series of narrow alleys, in a wonderful Newari quarter called **Mwana Tol**. Here there is a fine terrace of three-storeyed traditional houses overlooking an open space with its small *chaityas* and water-spout. Semi-private zones in front of each house are used for threshing, for stacking straw and drying produce. Do not pass through this area but continue past a corner *pathi*, a popular card-playing booth, and walk until you reach an impressive stone *shikhara* temple called **Lohan Dega**. Turn left and take note of the houses down this street. There will be great activity here as some of the most productive looms are located in the buildings on either side. Follow the pathway until you reach the next open square which should be in front of or close to the **Bagh Bhairab Temple**. This unusual rectangular temple, also built by Jagatpal Varma, hemmed in by a motley assortment of buildings, is the home of a celebrated but unusual image of Bhairab in his tiger form. It is arcaded at ground level and the walls bear some unusual paintings that are fast disappearing. The main door has a fine *torana* over it, with Vishnu riding Garuda over Bhairab flanked by Ganesh and Kumar. The upper levels have open balconies which are decorated with an assortment of swords and shields presented by the Newar warriors after their defeat by Prithvi Narayan Shah. Within the compound, there is an interesting collection of sculptures which are worth a glance.

In front of the temple is another large and supposedly very deep pond with a superb group of terraced houses, known as **Dev Phuku**, overlooking it. It is probable that they were owned at one time by an important Kirtipur leader. They are on flat ground and have extensive courtyards behind them.

To continue to the top of the town you must take the road that proceeds in a northwesterly direction alongside the entrance to the temple. After a zigzag, the path rises past some other impressive dwellings whose doors are decorated with a painted surround of Buddhist divinities. It leads you to another imposing structure with a fine but small five-bay window over a central door. This area is known as the **Lyakhu**, which defines it as part of the old Newari Palace—the likely centre of rule when Kirtipur was one of the lesser kingdoms of the Valley. The local people will explain that the high ground opposite this building was the main palace. The area has been somewhat disturbed by the erection of new buildings, but you will still see a vacant plot.

The end of this street is marked by two large and popular *pathis* between which you will find the steps to the temple on the hill. For years this temple remained derelict, but recently local efforts have undertaken a major renovation. The **Uma Maheswar Temple**, built in the 17th century, is locally called the **Kwatsa Dega**. It is dedicated to Shiva and Parvati but has little in the way of images to identify it. There is an unusual relic of past associations with the British, as a large bell proudly declares its Anglo-Saxon ancestry. From here, as you look over Kirtipur and beyond, you will appreciate that it is a compact urban settlement and you will realize how its natural fortifications made it the last stronghold of the Newars. Casting an eye over the fields below, you can understand what a thriving and wealthy farming community Kirtipur once was—today it is just a dormitory to the cities in the distance. After a moment's reflection, and if you are spurred on to further experiences on foot, descend the hill and pass behind it in a westerly direction.

If you need to return to the arrival point, retrace your steps to the Bagh Bhairab Temple and continue along the road on the left. You will reach the arrival point after walking a few minutes.

The Temples at Chobar Gorge

You are aiming now for **Chobar Adinath**, a temple on the next hill. The path follows a ridge route past an incomplete *stupa* known as **Majudega**. As you slowly ascend the hill towards the next hilltop, where Chobar Adinath is located, you will pass a small **temple to Vishnu Devi**. The compound inside has an assorted collection of sculptures. If you look among them you will notice there are images of Garuda, Saraswati, some devotees, and a stone pillar with Vaintej on top dated 1675.

You will shortly reach the **temple of Adinath** which, because of its location, is visible from afar. (If you wish to take the direct route to the temple from the road, you will find, a short distance beyond the entrance to the University, an archway and a flight of steps leading off into the distance. This path works its way up the Chobar hill directly to the compound.) The temple is a triple-roofed structure built originally in the 15th century, and enclosed in a monastic courtyard. Legends claim that the god Dharmaraj appeared to the Hindu king, Amsuvarman, and asked him to build a temple for him. The king's Buddhist advisers directed him to construct this temple at Chobar Adinath and to dedicate it to Lokeswar. You will notice that the temple is covered with an extraordinary collection of domestic utensils offered by newlyweds to ensure a happy and lasting marriage. Below the golden *torana* depicting six Buddhas, the masked face of a red Adinath Lokeswar peers from the main sanctum.

Facing this temple is the stone *shikhara* of **Gandeswar Bitrag** which, people say, hides an entrance to a passage which leads to the **Chobar cave** below. It would indeed be a nice way to reach the gorge which not so long ago was set in the most idyllic pastureland. Modern development has deemed that this pasture be torn open to extract limestone fo a cement factory just beyond the gorge.

Find your way as best you can to the beautiful suspension bridge imported from Glasgow and erected in 1903. From here you can view the narrow exit point of the Bagmati River. Sometimes serene, sometimes a rushing torrent, the river here finds its way out of the Valley, eventually to join the holy Ganga in the plains of India to the south. On the eastern bank, just beyond the gorge, is one of the four Ganesh shrines that protect the Valley. Those seeking strength of character will come to this simple three-tiered temple to pay homage to the massive rock—a small part of which looks like a tusk—that represents Ganesh. On the carved roof struts are some interesting details of Bhairab as well as Ganesh, with pretty damsels. The temple is encircled by pilgrims' quarters with direct access to the river, where you can see people milling along the banks.

You can follow the trail that leads beyond the bridge. This will take you through fields, across the ring road, into Patan via Jawalakhel.

Beyond Chobar and Kirtipur

An area often missed by explorers, though quite easily accessible, is the southwest corner beyond Chobar. Having passed the Chobar Gorge and the new cement factory, the road continues as far as the sacrificial site of Dakshinkali, a spot for the avid vampire.

Shortly after Chobar, there is an unusual lake on the left of the road known as **Taudaha Lake** which, legend relates, was created by Manjusri to provide a home for the *nags* which lived in the great Valley lake. The local people believe that the *nags* are still resident in the pond, and keep well away from it, making it a popular haunt for birdlife.

On the left-hand side of the road, as you drive along, you will see the old leprosarium of Kathmandu which has recently been rejuvenated by an aid organization. Some valiant work is being undertaken here to alleviate the suffering of many otherwise ostracized members of the community.

Just before you enter Pharping you may catch a glimpse of the first hydro-electric station in Nepal—the reservoir that drives the turbines is in Pharping. This system was introduced from England by the Ranas to provide electricity to the Singha Durbar, the seat of government at the beginning of this century. The power station is located close to the Bagmati River, and should you find yourself there late one evening just prior to the monsoon, your way will be lit by thousands of fireflies. It is a magical scene.

On the right of the road, just before you reach Pharping, is the summit of **Champa Devi**. It is another pleasant climb to this landmark, once described as 'two-tree' and then 'one-tree' hill (because of an alleged distinctive pair of trees on its summit, although whether they exist anymore is a matter of doubt). Criminals, it is said, were hanged from one of the trees.

Below is the village of **Pharping** which the road will shortly reach. This settlement has two interesting shrines, one in the village and one just above it. Should you climb Champa Devi, it is possible to descend via the **Bajrayogini shrine** of Pharping. Otherwise, beyond Pharping you will find a path that merges with a flight of steps which leads up to the temple complex. At the head of the stairs is the small enclosed compound of the three-tiered temple. There are also two wings of pilgrims' quarters, one on either side of the entrance. The temple was constructed in the 17th century. The main sanctum on the upper floor houses Bajrayogini. In the sanctum below is a collection of other divinities, among them Avaloketeswar, Basundara and Sakyamuni. As can be expected, this site was occupied by sages and holy men who spent time in meditation here.

Further up the hillock, beyond the Bajrayogini shrine, is a narrow terrace in front of the entrance to a cave. Its location is indicated by a colourful array of prayer-flags strung from the trees. Legend tells that Padma Sambhava stayed in this cave on his way from India to Tibet. In a *chaitya* close by, there is also an imprint of Goraknath's foot with an inscription dating from 1390. The caves are visited by people of all religions but it is mostly frequented by Tibetans and followers of Northern Lamaism.

Below, at the entrance to Pharping, is an interesting group of sculptures amid a series of clear pools and a cave shrine dedicated to Sekh Narayan. Most of the statues relate to Vishnu's incarnations, although there are a few representing Shiva. Some, like the 13th-century Surya image, are set into or at the edge of the pools, creating interesting illusions as the large fish inhabiting the ponds swirl around them. The shrine has been an important place of pilgrimage since the 15th century.

At the end of the road is **Dakshinkali**, the scene of mass slaughter to Kali. Every Tuesday and Saturday, more animals are offered in sacrifice at this spot than anywhere else in the Valley. The main divinity was brought here, so it is said, by King Pratap Malla in the 17th century on the orders of the goddess herself. He therefore enshrined a fearsome black image of Kali trampling a male human. For pilgrims, a trip to Dakshinkali is an excuse for a family outing as, after their sacrifice to propitiate the gods, they will picnic on the grassy slopes around the shrine overlooking the rivulets that run down through the gorge. There is no doubt that the location has a very sinister atmosphere, which even curious tourists cannot break. Slightly above the main shrine there is a simple and peaceful temple dedicated to the Mother Goddess.

Although the Bagmati River finds its way into the lowlands of Nepal from here, and despite plans to find a quicker route to the Terai, this is the end of the road. From here you must retrace your tracks to Kathmandu.

The Twin Towns of Khokana and Bungamati

About 12 kilometres (seven and a half miles) to the south of Patan, via Jawalakhel, are the two towns of Khokana and Bungamati set in the most beautiful part of the Valley and surrounded by richly endowed paddy fields. It is well worth spending half a day exploring these unspoilt settlements and walking through the lush and fertile fields.

Khokana

The towns are accessible off the ring road beyond Jawalakhel, south of Patan. A dirt road drops down from the main road past an infamous jail to reach a small hamlet adjacent to the Nakhu Khola, a small river that leads into the Bagmati. A large girder bridge formerly spanned this tributary but floods washed away its foundations. It is possible to cross the river using a new bridge. However, there is a pleasant walk along the river bank on foot. Eventually, you will come across a well-defined path that will bring you to the main road at the turn-off point to Khokana. If you manage to cross the river, continue along the road for about three kilometres (two miles) and you will reach the turn-off point to Khokana. There is a tumbledown *pathi* at the top of a fairly steep road that descends towards the town. Follow the road until you reach a large, walled tank marking the entrance to Khokana. From here on, you step back into the Middle Ages as you witness simple village life in rural Nepal. During the grain-drying seasons, the route will be lined by tonnes of wheat or rice spread out to dry or being winnowed by scores of womenfolk in their red-edged, black sari-style dresses hitched high over their ankles to show their delicate tattoos. In the ponds, the women wash themselves and their clothes in the murky water using a clay-like substance as soap. At the second pond, take the higher path and shortly you will pass a dimly lit oil-press—a truly mediaeval sight—where men struggle to turn a wheel that is geared to large baulks of timber between which the triangular woven bamboo containers of cooked mustard seed are pressed to extract oil. The half-naked bodies of the operators glisten with sweat and oil. These are members of the Manandhar caste.

Follow the stone-paved route until it opens out on the right to the unusually wide main street which, after damage in the 1934 earthquake, was broadened when rebuilt. The street is always full of activity, a *mélange* of animals and drying crops, often divided by long lines of women setting the warps ready for weaving their local cloth. At the bottom end of the street, the main **temple of Rudrayani** stands sentinel over these activities. A crowd of children will lead you further down and show you a beautiful near-lifesize sculpture of Manjusri set among a group of *pathis*. The street narrows and continues towards the steep descent to the Bagmati River. Follow the path a short way and then turn left and seek the path that leads behind Khokana towards Bungamati in a southerly direction. Follow the main trail as it runs through the paddy fields for about half an hour and then climb towards Bungamati. Farmers working in the fields will be happy to show you the way.

Bungamati

You enter Bungamati through the back streets and soon you will find yourself in a large and impressive open square with an unusually large, white stuccoed *Shikhara*-style temple on a stone base in the centre. This is the second home of the Rato Machhendra, when it is not residing in Patan.

Bungamati is said to have been established by King Narendradev in 1593 and it is he who also started the tradition of the Machhendra festival here. The village is smaller and more compact than Khokana, and life revolves around the brick-paved temple square which is scattered with small Buddhist *chaityas* and prayer-wheels. Again this unusual open space is used by the inhabitants as an extension of their dwellings and for tethering their livestock. During the festival period at the beginning and end of the deity's residence in Bungamati, this courtyard is the scene of great activity and every 12th year

(the next is in 2003) the juggernaut-sized chariot will be hauled all the way from Patan and back to this square, transporting the divinity to its new resting place (see page 171).

In the southeastern corner there is a small but important temple and *dyochhen* dedicated to Bhairab, with its sanctum on the second floor accessible up an open staircase.

Leaving the square by the northern entrance, spare a moment to look back at the gate and the group of lions on guard. Along this path, to the left, you will pass a pond and a small but unusual *bahal* known as **Bunga Bahil**. Shortly afterwards, the street opens up and you take a left turn towards Khokana, out on to the paddy fields. A broad path leads straight to the entrance of Khokana, passing on the way the **Kara Binayak Shrine**. A path to it leads off to the left, up on to a beautiful clearing and a small walled compound. Here you will find a small but heavily gilded **shrine to Ganesh**. The stone is a natural rendition of the elephant god and is much revered by those who have difficult tasks to accomplish. It is also a popular holiday picnic spot.

Return to the path through the fields and you will recognize the main road coming down the hill to Khokana from where this journey into the past began.

Beyond the Kathmandu Valley

In the early days of mountaineering, when there were virtually no roads even in the Kathmandu Valley, expeditions used to walk from the Valley, sometimes taking two or three weeks to reach their base camps. Today, with the ever-increasing mileage of hard-top roads, there are plenty of opportunities to see, either by driving or flying, several destinations beyond the rim of the Valley.

Most travellers who have the time will head off into the mountains to one of several destinations for a trek lasting either a few days or a few weeks. The two most popular trail heads are either **Pokhara**—a town six hours' drive through spectacular terraced scenery in the lower highlands of Nepal; or **Lukhla** in the Solu Khumbu region of the Himalaya from where the treks to Everest begin. While Lukhla is only for trekkers, as it is necessary to fly there (or walk for a week!), in Pokhara it is possible for anyone to spend a few days enjoying the spectacular mountain scenery, for here Macchapucchare, the Fishtail Mountain, dominates the Himalayan backdrop and can be viewed across the Phewa Lake. From Pokhara, where the many hotels range from the semi-luxurious to the basic trekkers' lodge, you can spend dreamy days along the lake's edge or set off for walks into the hills to visit the nearby Tibetan refugee camp.

Another trail head is **Trisuli Bazaar** located a few hours' drive to the northwest of Kathmandu. The road continues beyond Trisuli to **Betrawati** which is the starting point for the Langtang Trails. Historically, Trisuli is an important town as just above it in the **Palace of Nuwakot**, King Prithvi Narayan Shah planned the conquest of the Kathmandu Valley in 1769. The palace, which is accessible by road, commands magnificent views over the surrounding country and in itself is an interesting structure. It is said to be the forerunner of the Basantapur Tower in the Hanuman Dhoka and has, as its name implies, nine storeys. The road to Trisuli is dramatic and passes several view points. One that is only 45 minutes from Kathmandu is **Kakani** from where there are magnificent views towards the Ganesh Himal.

Deep in the **Terai** or lowlands of Nepal and close to the Indian border on the plains of Kapilavastu is **Lumbini**, the birthplace of the Buddha. Lumbini is about 250 kilometres (155 miles) from Kathmandu and is accessible by road via Pokhara and Bhairawa or by air via Bhairawa. Lumbini and the district are undergoing a massive change and update as provisions are being made for 20th-century pilgrims following the masterplan of the famous Japanese architect Kenzo Tange. However, the famous **shrine of the Maya Devi**, with an image depicting the Buddha's nativity, is said to be at the spot where his birth occurred. The town in which his parents lived is the present archaeological site of **Tilaurakot** about 25 kilometres (16 miles) west of Lumbini. This part of the Terai certainly has an air of peace and tranquillity

Birdwatching in the Kathmandu Valley

by Toby Sinclair

Although highly populated and well cultivated, the Valley and surrounding hills are rich in birdlife. With an average altitude at 1,330 metres (4,365 feet), and the nearby hills of Pulchowki, Sheopuri and Nagarjung ranging from 2,105–2,760 metres (6,900–9,055 feet), the wide variety of habitat and altitude in the Valley make even casual birdwatching particularly rewarding. The Flemings in their book *The Birds of Nepal* list over 400 bird species here and have recorded up to 180 in a single day!

Almost anywhere in the Valley can be easily reached from Kathmandu. In order to get to an area before dawn, a taxi booked the previous evening would be easiest but fixed bus routes do pass some areas and others are close enough to cycle to. Bicycles can be hired by the day or week but are not advisable if Pulchowki is your objective.

October, March and April are the most interesting months with great concentrations of migratory species arriving or departing. However a day's birdwatching at any time of year is worthwhile. If you are going out of the Valley on a trek for a couple of weeks or more, a few day's birdwatching in the Valley both before and after your trek will probably reveal a variety of species. The best time is early morning although the Valley is often covered in mist until 9 am in December and January. During the summer it tends to get too hot by midday.

Sadly most of the forest ringing the valley has been cut down over the last 30 years or so and the demand for fuel, fodder and timber continues. Nevertheless some areas remain and a few are protected. One of the best places to start observing the Valley's extensive bird life is on the southern rim. At the Royal Botanical gardens in Godaveri, 25 minutes drive south of Kathmandu, some of the original subtropical forest has been preserved. The gardens are open from 9 am to 5 pm but are best avoided on Saturdays and public holidays. Originally developed by some experts from Kew, the gardens have a mix of endemic and introduced species which support a varied bird population. The tallest of the hills encircling the valley is Pulchowki, meaning 'flower-covered hill', which rises to 2,762 metres (9,062 feet) above Godaveri. A small shrine at its summit is dedicated to Pulchowki Mai, the mother of the forest. The summit is not only the begining of a good birdwatching walk but also commands spectacular views of the Valley and the Himalaya to the north. For the birdwatcher it is best to drive straight to the summit, walk slowly back down the road and then follow one of the woodcutters' trails down the lower slopes to Godaveri. Black-capped sibias, red-headed laughing-thrushes and other songbirds in the oak forest near the top give a lively welcome at the start. A few hundred metres below the summit, black-throated parrotbills are often seen in the bamboo.

Recently established on the northern side of the valley, 12 kilometres (7.5 miles) north of Kathmandu, is the Sheopuri Wildlife Reserve. A track leads through the village of Budhanilkantha (see page 100), over a bridge crossing a stream and up to the reserve's boundary wall. A gate leads into the reserve. The climb to the summit at 2,730 metres (8,956 feet) takes almost four hours, but a relaxed walk through the thick secondary scrub on the lower slopes and the good forest slightly higher offers plenty of species. In February and March the lower slopes of Sheopuri are one of the easiest places to see the spiney babbler, Nepal's only truly endemic bird species.

A third forested hillside at Nagarjung is only five kilometres (three miles) northwest of Kathmandu beyond Balaju. The hill is enclosed by a boundary wall and it is best to drive to the Jamachok summit at 2,105 metres (6,900 feet) and walk down through the woods.

A small forested hill rising to 1,385 metres (4,543 feet) at Gokarna three kilometres (two miles) east of Baudhanath is now a safari park. As with Godaveri, it is best avoided on Saturdays and holidays. Part of the forest still has plenty of old trees with the occasional brown fish owl or brown wood owl roosting near the top.

Apart from the few protected areas of forest there are still some other areas of relatively undisturbed stretches along the Bagmati and Manora rivers which attract migrant waders and duck. The stretch of the Bagmati near Basant Gaon, five kilometres (three miles) south of Kathmandu, and the Chobar Gorge (through which the waters of the Kathmandu Lake were released by Manjusri), are particularly good in March–April and August–November. The protected woods near Pashupatinath and Swayambhu are also good for flycatchers, minevets and other woodland birds.

The Nepal Birdwatching Club has regular field meetings and can be contacted care of Victoria's Travels and Tours, PO Box 536, Kamaladi, Kathmandu (tel 226130; fax 224237).

which, it is hoped, the new development will not disturb.

Another place worth a visit is the old royal town of **Gorkha**—the former seat of the Shah Dynasty before their conquest of the Kathmandu Valley. Half-way between Kathmandu and Pokhara a recently completed black-top road leads to the **lower palace of Gorkha**, a large courtyard building dating from the early 17th century, which is undergoing conservation and conversion to a museum. Set on a ridge overlooking the town is the famous **Gorkha palace** founded in the 15th century. It has recently undergone considerable restoration and is now enclosed by an extensive boundary wall; previously its strategic location provided sufficient protection. It takes a long hour to walk up the several thousand steps to the palace, but from it the views towards the Himalaya and across the countryside are spectacular. However, the military reception at the palace could be friendlier: no information is available, while photography and the carrying of umbrellas are forbidden!

For the safari buff there is the thrill of viewing wildlife from atop an elephant and jungle walks in the **Royal Chitwan National Park**. Many jungle lodges, such as Machan, Temple Tiger, and Tiger Tops, to name but a few, arrange transport from Kathmandu to the jungle where you are met by elephant and transported in style to your lodge. Here an intensive few days of wildlife safari on elephants (not native to the park), birdwatching on foot, and camping under the stars, awaits you—at a price. For those on a stricter budget a wide choice of accommodation is available in the immediate vicinity of the park. For the adventurous, an extended white-water river trip can be arranged through many different rafting organizations.

For a wonderful way to see the Kathmandu Valley and Nepal contact biker James Giambrone of **Himalayan Mountain Bikes** by phone or fax at (977-1) 411724. James runs a bicycle trekking company which supplies bikes, guides, and full support from a one-day to a two-week trip.

Nepal has a good network of local flights with airports of airstrips scattered throughout the kingdom. It is possible to reach **Phaphlu**, or **Jomsom** in the mountains, or **Nepalgunj** or **Janakpur** in the Terai; but the return journey may not be quite so easy and only those with plenty of spare time are advised to go beyond the standard tourist routes; the fickle mountain weather can disrupt even the best-laid plans.

Crafts and Artifacts of the Kathmandu Valley

Apart from building crafts, which have been described at some length, a wealth of handicrafts is to be found in the Kathmandu Valley. Besides the metalcrafts, woodcarvings and religious paintings which were the crafts mainly associated with religion and religious festivals, tourism has popularized handmade fabrics and jewellery which can now be bought in the bazaars.

There is also a thriving antique market and anything considered 'old' is expensive. Do not be taken in by the street vendors, who will sell you carved ivory Chinese figurines produced out of an oily rag at knock-down prices—these are mass-produced resin-bonded plastic specimens from Hong Kong. Also be wary of the ancient brass Buddhas aged with bootblack that have barely had time to cool. In fact, you should be wary of all possible antiques, even in the smartest shops, as age is greatly exaggerated. If you do find an old piece you must have it certified for export by the Department of Archaeology (in Ramshahpath). However, the bazaars and the shops along Durbar Marg, New Road and in Thamel are full of enticing bargains. Much of the older material you will find comes from, or is inspired by, the people of the Himalayan regions or of Tibet. You will find some beautiful brass and copper objects, mostly of a religious nature, some of which are of extremely high quality. *Thangkas* or religious paintings are also popular souvenirs. Quality varies tremendously and much importance is give by the vendor to the amount of gold or silver included in the design. Check on the fineness of the detail—some of the paintings are extremely intricate—and do not be fooled by the mellow look of the pieces. Most of the paintings are 'smoked' to give them a patina of age.

In the **Basantapur market** you will find hundreds of curio dealers with their open-air shops selling everything from beautiful traditional wooden honey pots to plastic junk from Hong Kong. For the discerning eye, many a happy bargain can be struck.

The rag trade has hit Kathmandu in a big way. There are tailors hidden in every corner, who can run up the latest fashions at remarkably cheap rates. As the old adage goes, 'you get what you pay for'. The original woollen jacket decorated with braids was a Swiss inspiration to develop the handicraft market and it heralded the beginning of several new styles and an exciting new fashion. It was soon followed by the sweater fashion which is now a popular cottage industry and, like the braided shoulder bag, has become the stamp of a visitor to Nepal.

Some of the more traditional souvenirs, such as the wool and *pashmina* shawls or the traditional Newari-style jewellery, are excellent buys. You can spend hours in the **Bead Market**, buy scores of beautiful necklaces and find that your bill will amount to only a few dollars! In many places you can find well-crafted, inexpensive jewellery—rings, earrings, bracelets—some with semi-precious stones in silver settings.

Traditional masks of highly painted papier mâché represent incarnations of the divinities. They are colourful reminders of the Valley and are easily transportable. Another attractive craft, but not so portable, are the terracotta pots and animals which are in abundant use everywhere. They are very well made and temptingly cheap.

The carpet industry is undoubtedly the fastest growing and most prolific of all the handicraft industries in Nepal. The generic Tibetan carpet made in Nepal is a very popular souvenir and there are hundreds of shops and thousands of designs to choose from. The traditional Tibetan carpet adorned the seats of temples and the beds of houses and today these old and mature carpets are collector's pieces. It is possible to find some of the traditional designs and colours— vegetable-dye carpets are the rage—but modern designs and pastel shades are the more favoured export models. The quality of carpet depends on the type of wool used, the way it is spun and the number of knots per square inch.

Do not be fooled into thinking that the Kashmiri handicrafts are Nepali or made in Nepal. They are imported into Nepal and are expensive compared with similar pieces available in, for instance, Delhi.

Shopping in Nepal is an exciting and enjoyable pastime. Through your bargaining sessions you will have a chance to meet and learn a little about the Nepalis and their traditions. You will also collect some wonderful mementoes of the Kathmandu Valley, though the memory of striking the bargain may last longer than the actual purchase!

Festivals

The many different festivals that take place every year form an important part of life in Nepal. As the Nepalis use the Nepali calendar, the Bikram Samvat, which does not tally with the Christian calendar, the dates on which they fall according to the latter vary from year to year. In view of this the festivals have been arranged below according to the month they may fall in.

Hardly a week goes by without some festival taking place in Nepal. However, whether local or national in character, most of them are associated with one or other of the divinities sacred to either Hindu or Buddhist theology or mythology. All festivals are celebrated with the same verve by both religions, each possibly worshipping different facets of the same god as suits its individual dogma.

Religious Festivals

Magh (January/February)

Basant Panchami

This festival celebrates the arrival of Spring. On this day, the goddess of learning, Saraswati, is worshipped, especially by students who are about to take their exams. Thousands of people flock to the Saraswati shrine in Swayambhu, after which they picnic in large groups on the grassy slopes below the *stupa* there. In Hanuman Dhoka, the king goes in procession to the Nasal Chowk to hear a recital of songs of Spring in which prayers are offered for a good return of crops in the midst of a colourful ceremony that is held beneath a specially erected canopy.

Falgun (February/March)

Shivaratri

This is perhaps one of the most spectacular festivals of the year and attracts many thousands of people from all over Nepal and the northern parts of India. A great fair or *mela* is held in Pashupatinath, to which an amazing cross-section of the different races and tribes of Nepal and India flock to pay homage at the most important shrine in Nepal. The worshippers aim at arriving the night before—several in fact arrive in the Valley days or weeks before to shop and explore—to prepare for their ritual bath in the holy Bagmati River which runs through the temple complex. After their symbolic dip, they line up in colourful queues to make their offerings to Lord Pashupati, the protector of the Kathmandu Valley. The rest of the day is spent in feasting, singing and dancing. At this time, the environs of Pashupatinath are teeming with people; street traders swarm on the place to sell their wares, be it fruit, flowers, clothing or toys—there is even a bit of government propa-

ganda for health services and family planning. The roads are lined with beggars and a colourful collection of *sadhus*—holy men from India scantily clad in makeshift loincloths, their bodies smeared with ashes, their uncut and unwashed hair piled high upon the head in a topknot. These visitors are provided with food and firewood as a courtesy by the Nepal Government.

The best time to visit Pashupatinath is shortly after dawn when the worshippers shed their old clothes and plunge into the freezing waters, soon to emerge and don new clothes, the women bedecking themselves in beautiful red and gold saris before paying homage in the temple. This ocean of colour is one of the most beautiful sights imaginable, especially as the sun penetrates the mist rising off the river. The evening gatherings around wood fires and the traditional folk-singing add a different dimension to the festival. Elsewhere in the Valley, large bonfires are lit at major crossroads to ward off evil spirits and to protect those undertaking the night-long vigil.

Holi

This is often referred to as the 'Festival of Colour' and is of Indian Hindu tradition. It is a week of fun and revelry, especially among children who shower each other with coloured water throughout the week. The festival culminates in a 'dangerous' day when rubber balloons filled with coloured water are thrown at unsuspecting passers-by, all in the name of fun! The only ritual is at the beginning of the week and is the erection in the Basantapur Square of a bamboo pole decorated with a colourful mass of streamers. To mark the end of the festival, the pole is taken down and burnt.

Chaitra (March/April)

Ghodajatra

This was originally a Newari festival centred on feasting with friends and worshipping Bhadrakali and Kankeshwari, whose images are paraded through the narrow streets of Asan the night before the festival. At the same time, the demon Gurumpa is feasted on the Tundikhel. However, today Ghodajatra is noted for its competitive sports such as horse-racing and cycling and a display by the army which take place on the Tundikhel. It is a spectacular military pageant.

Chaitra Dasain and Seto Machhendranath

These are two separate festivals which occur around the same time. Chaitra Dasain is timed to be exactly six months before the Maha Ashtami day during the festival of Dasain in late September. It is a day when sacrificial offerings are made to Durga in a ritual that takes place at midday, as opposed to midnight during Dasain. Chaitra Dasain marks the start of the Kathmandu *rath* festival. The Seto Machhendra image is taken from its shrine in Machhendra Bahal, off Asan Tol, and is placed in a towering chariot (*rath*) to be trundled through the streets of old Kathmandu. The festival takes four days to complete, the chariot stopping at specific places each night where the image is worshipped and cared for by the people of that locality. The chariot, which is towed on 1.8-metre (six foot) -diameter wheels by hundreds of young boys, is spectacular, particularly as it dwarfs the buildings on the streets through which it passes. It is usually moved in the early evening. On the final day, the chariot is dragged around a tree in Lagan Khel, after which the deity is transported back to its temple on a small palanquin.

Baisakh (April/May)

Bisket

This festival is special to Bhaktapur and is perhaps one of the most exciting and frenetic of all the major public festivals in Nepal. During the mid-April, week-long celebrations, the goddesses of Bhairab and Bhadrakali are paraded in chariots throughout the town. The revels start with a major trial of strength between the inhabitants of the eastern and western halves of the town in a tug-of-war of surprising dimensions. They begin in the square beneath the Nyatapola Temple around dusk. The challenge is to settle who is to play host to the main deity during the festivities. A five-metre (16-foot) -high chariot is built in the centre of the square and two long ropes, one attached to each end of the chariot, are run out along the main streets of the square. The deity is installed and, while she is protected by her guardian priests, each half of the town, fuelled by large quantities of local beer, endeavours forcibly to drag the chariot into its own territory. This battle continues throughout the night, until one side retires from exhaustion and accepts defeat. To witness this festival it is best to go in the company of one of the townsfolk as the participants often get a little out of control in their endeavour to win the honour of being hosts to the god.

The second stage of the proceedings is to escort the deity to the banks of the river down a steep and twisting road. This is a somewhat dangerous undertaking as the passage of the chariot is often hampered by the surging crowds or even a building which may have collapsed in its path. Once the chariot reaches the bank of the river, a long pole is raised vertically to commemorate victory during the great battle described in the *Mahabharata* (see pages 108–9). The following day, the pole, which is of considerable length, is felled to signify the beginning of the Nepali new year. To give the losers of the tug-of-war a chance to wash away the ignominy of their earlier defeat, a return match is held at the end of the festival, by which time, it is hoped, their opponents will be handicapped by their excessive feasting!

Rato Machhendranath Jatra (Samek)

This chariot festival is one of the major festivals of Patan and is similar to the *rath* festival held in Kathmandu. The main difference is that it lasts a month or so and the chariot is very much larger. The deity is shared with the village of Bungamati, to the southeast of Patan, and every 12th year (the next is 2003) the chariot itself has to be taken there. This is a major undertaking as the road is very hilly and far from smooth. Each year, however, the deity spends three months in Bungamati but in the intervening years it is carried there on a palanquin.

The festival is launched in Pulchok where the chariot is reconstructed each year and for about a month it wends its way precariously through the streets of Patan. Because of its immense size, a contingent from the army is called upon to assist in pulling the chariot to each new destination. The culmination of the festival is at Jawalakhel when the historic bejewelled tunic, supposedly belonging to the serpent king, is publicly displayed on the auspicious day of Boto Jatra, in the presence of His Majesty the King. The festival aims at ensuring that there will be a satisfactory monsoon for the coming rice crop. During the celebrations, a coconut is flung down from the chariot's pinnacle, bringing good fortune to the lucky devotee who manages to catch it.

Buddha Jayanti

As the Lord Buddha was born in Lumbini in the southern Terai of Nepal, his birthday is celebrated with great veneration throughout the country. Special ceremonies take place at the major Buddhist sites of Swayambhu and Baudha, with both processions and large prayer gatherings in the neighbouring monasteries. Pilgrims come from all over Nepal to these sites to celebrate the day and they make a very colourful spectacle. Great gatherings take place in Baudhanath and Swayambhu, and proceedings are conducted with much pomp, especially by the Tibetan monks who herald them with giant Tibetan horns. Prayer flags are raised in rainbows of colour and costumed monks enact festive dances. At night, thousands of butter-lamps flicker around the bases of the great *stupas*. Tibetans in their thousands descend from everywhere in pilgrimage to the great *stupa* of Baudhanath.

Srawan (July/August)

Janai Purnima

This festival mainly concerns Brahmins but most other Hindus also participate. On this day, Brahmins bathe in the sacred rivers of the Vishnumati and the Bagmati, after which they change the sacred threads worn across their chest. Other people have yellow sacred threads tied round their wrist to protect them from the dangers of the coming year. On this day, thousands of people visit the Kumbeswar Temple in Patan where they bathe in the sacred

waters which supposedly come from the holy lakes in Gosainkund set at over 3,700 metres (12,000 feet) in the foothills to the northeast of the Kathmandu Valley. The precincts of Kumbeswar in Patan present a colourful spectacle during this festival as, after their symbolical cleansing, the throngs of people pay homage to the beautiful gold and silver *lingam* which is usually kept in the temple but on this day is placed on a platform in the middle of the tank.

Bhadra (August/September)

Gaijatra

This festival, akin to a carnival, is celebrated in Kathmandu, Patan and Bhaktapur, with only slight variations on a central theme. Families in which deaths have occurred during the previous year send a cow, or a young child masquerading as a cow, in procession around the streets of the city as a tribute to the deceased and to assist their entry into heaven. This procession takes place during the morning and is followed in the afternoon by a further, more carnival-like procession, when participants mimic the social and political scene of the day. The processions staged in Bhaktapur are perhaps the most extensive and amusing, with a wide range of tableaux typifying all aspects of the people's culture. The festival lasts about eight days, the first and second day being the most important. On the second day, an important Buddhist festival known as **Mataya** takes place, when all the *viharas* (Buddhist monasteries or temples) of Patan are visited in sequence. As there are as many as 150 of them, this is a formidable undertaking. Offerings are made by the pilgrims and butter-lamps are lit along the route.

Teej-Brata

This three-day festival is especially observed by women. It consists of a period of fasting and a ritual cleansing in the Bagmati River. Women, dressed in their finery, flock to Pashupati to bathe in the river and afterwards to worship at the shrine of Lord Pashupati, creating a very colourful spectacle along the river bank.

Gokarna Aunshi (Father's Day)

This is a father's day celebration which is highlighted by ritual bathing in the Bagmati River beneath the Gokarna Mahadev Temple by families whose fathers have died during the last year. Living fathers are presented with gifts by their offspring and picnics are held along the river bank.

Krishna Astami

A festival celebrating the birth of Krishna takes place at all the important shrines dedicated to him. In particular, at the Krishna Mandir Temple in Patan, there is a beautiful festival in the evening when women and girls make offerings of special flowers and sing challenging love duets with their male admirers—a kind of romantic banter.

Indrajatra

This is perhaps one of the most important and certainly the most spectacular of all Nepali festivals, celebrated by Hindus and Buddhists alike. It lasts for about eight days, during which time there is much rejoicing, dancing and ceremony. On the first day a long pole is erected close to Hanuman Dhoka to propitiate Indra, the god of rain. After its erection there is a colourful display of classical dancing by masked dancers. On the third day, Kumari, the living goddess, a young girl selected from the Sakye caste is brought out into the streets in her special chariot, accompanied by her attendants, Ganesh and Bhairab, in smaller chariots, who are represented by two young boys. It is on this day that the King, who attends the festivities, is entertained by the masked dancers and pays homage to Kumari. All over the cities, wooden masks of Bhairab are exhibited and at certain times of the day local beer pours forth from their mouths through a spout to revive local revellers. Indra, with his arms outstretched, can also be seen set atop a high platform. History records that it was on this day that King Prithvi Narayan Shah conquered Kathmandu and unified Nepal. Many public recitals of classical dance and religious tableaux are staged in the Kathmandu Durbar Square.

Ashwin (September/October)

Durga Puja—Dasain

Durga Puja, or Dasain, is the national festival of Nepal and lasts 15 days. It is a time for family reunion and rejoicing; therefore, most of the festival's activities take place within the family group as it is often the only time during the year when the whole family is together. The basic theme of the festival is the conquest of evil. Legend has it that during the time of this festival, Ram Chandra vanquished Ravana of Lanka. On **Phulpati**, the day of flowers, there is a colourful procession to Hanuman Dhoka attended by the king.

The following day, **Maha Ashtami**, Durga is fêted and thousands of buffaloes and goats are sacrificed at shrines all over the country, symbolizing the cleansing of the soul. It is on this day that the Taleju shrines in the main cities are opened to the faithful and throughout the night thousands of pilgrims flock to pay homage. The following days are spent in family gatherings and, on Bijaya Dasami, relatives visit their elders for blessing and *tikka*.

Kartik (October/November)

Tihar (Diwali)

Celebrated over a period of five days, this festival is often called Diwali, as in India. Various animals and gods are worshipped and houses are illuminated at night with hundreds of candles and butter-lamps. Sadly, in the main cities, these are being replaced by electric lights. On the first day, the crow, which symbolizes Yama Duta the messenger of death, is called to the house and fed. Dogs are fêted and garlanded on the second day, as they are the mounts of Bhairab. On the third day, the cow—as an incarnation of Laxmi, the goddess of wealth and prosperity—is worshipped, and on the last day, brothers are fêted with garlands and sweetmeats by their sisters who are in turn rewarded with money. Every evening Laxmi is paid special attention and her footprints, traced by worshippers, lead to their safes or treasure boxes. During this period, the Newari new year is celebrated with much feasting and gambling.

National Festivals

Throughout the year there are also several national festivals commemorating historical and regal events in Nepal. The most important ones are listed below.

Falgun (February/March)

Democracy Day

This day celebrates the overthrow of the Rana regime in 1951, when King Tribhuvan returned from his self-imposed exile in India to re-establish Nepal as a democratic kingdom. Parades and processions are held, especially on the Tundikhel in Kathmandu.

Asadh (July/August)

Tribhuvan Jayanti

This is a national day to commemorate His Late Majesty, King Tribhuvan, the present King's grandfather. The ceremony takes place around his statue in Tripureswar.

Margh (November/December)

Constitution Day

On this day every town in Nepal commemorates the 1962 Constitutional Act. Tribute is paid to the late King Mahendra, the father of the present monarch, who established modern-day Nepal.

The Birthday of His Majesty King Birendra

King Birendra Bir Bikram Shah Dev was born on 28 December 1945. On his birthday each year there are extensive military parades and processions throughout the kingdom.

Practical Information

Kathmandu Hotels

There has been a steady increase in the number of hotels in the Kathmandu Valley as more and more tourists come. Many of the older hotels have extended their capacity. Most of the hotels are adequately appointed and even the cheapest often have attached bathrooms. In many places hot water is heated by solar panels on the roof. The five-star hotels match European standards and where this is lacking it is certainly made up for by the friendliness of the staff.

A few hotels are converted old buildings. Although they provide that added local dimension of tradition, they fall short of full Western comfort. The hotel Shanker is housed in an old Rana palace; Dwarika's is a specially designed village hotel incorporating some of the finest woodcarvings in the Kathmandu Valley; and part of the Kathmandu Guest House is housed in a converted old building of character.

Listed below are all the major hotels located in the Kathmandu Valley and some of the more popular smaller and less expensive haunts of the zealous traveller.

Deluxe

Yak and Yeti, Durbar Marg (central location). Tel: 222635, 413999. Fax: 227782. 270 rooms, 23 suites. Has pool, shops, tennis, casino etc

Soaltee Holiday Inn Crowne Plaza, Kalimati (outside city centre), Tel: 272550, 272555. Fax: 272205. 300 rooms, 7 regal and 4 standard suites. Casino, pool, tennis.

Annapurna, Durbar Marg (central location). Tel: 221711. Fax: 225236. 160 rooms, 4 suites. Has pool, shops, tennis, casino etc.

Everest, Naya Baneswar (on road to airport). Tel: 220567, 220389. Fax: 226088, 224421. 162 rooms, 6 suites. Has pool, tennis, health club, shops, casino etc.

Shangri-la, Lazimpat (NE of city centre). Tel: 412999, 410108. Fax: 414184. 82 rooms, 4 suites, beautiful garden. Has shops, pool etc.

Shanker, Lazimpat (NE of city centre). Tel: 410151, 410152. Fax: 412691. 94 rooms, 10 suites, has large garden.

First Class
Malla, Lainchaur (close to Royal Palace). Tel: 410966, 410620. Fax: 418382. 97 rooms, fine apartments. Has gardens, shops and pool.

Himalaya, Kupondol (on way to Patan gate). Tel: 523900. Fax: 523909. 100 rooms, 3 suites. Has pool, tennis, badminton, large lobby, good mountain views.

Narayani, Pulchowk, Patan. Tel: 521711, 525015, 525018. Fax: 521291. 87 rooms, 4 suites. Has pool. Health club with squash and tennis courts nearby.

Sherpa, Durbar Marg (central location). Tel: 227000, 228889. Fax: 222026. 87 rooms, 6 suites. Has pool.

Kathmandu, Maharajganj (well NE of the city centre). Tel: 418494, 418495, 418497. Fax: 414091, 416574. 82 rooms, 2 suites.

Second Class
Yellow Pagoda, Kantipath (central location). Tel: 220392, 220337, 220338. Fax: 228914. 57 rooms.

Dwarika's, Batisputali (out of town, near airport). Tel: 472328, 470770. Fax: 471379. 31 rooms. Has fine setting amid beautiful carvings.

Ambassador, Lazimpat (NE of city centre, on way to British Embassy). Tel: 414432, 410432, 419432. Fax: 413641. Friendly place, moderately priced.

Kathmandu Guest House, Thamel (central location). Tel: 413632, 418733. Fax: 417379. Includes garden. Popular with world travellers. Wide price range starting from US$5 per night.

The Summit, Kupondol Height, Patan (out of town). Tel: 521894, 524694, 521810 Fax: 523737. 47 rooms. Beautifully designed with local materials. Summit tower. Recently opened long-stay apartments with stunning mountain views.

Vajra, (on the road to Swayambhu, west of town) Tel: 271545, 271824, 272719. Fax: 271695. 40 rooms. Has rooftop restaurant and bar. Unusual cultural experience.

Taragaon, Bodhanath. Tel: 470409, 470413. 17 rooms. Overlooks stupa. Has detached units. Plans in hand for major extension.

Others
There are plenty of other reasonably priced places to stay in and around Thamel or in Freak Street, now no longer frequented by hippies at the end of the overland trail. A short walk is certain to turn up something, and grumpy hotel staff are virtually unknown in Kathmandu as competition is intense.

Food

The staple diet of the Nepalis in the Valley is rice, lentils and vegetables liberally spiced with garlic, red peppers and turmeric. Once a week, meat may be eaten—either chicken, goat or buffalo. In the hands of a good cook this can be a gastronomic delight, but otherwise it is rather uninteresting. During their festivals the Newars produce magnificent banquets, which often feed hundreds of their clan mambers, and include a great assortment of dishes. Every scrap of the sacrificial animal will be served up as a different delicacy.

The Nepalis themselves generally prefer their own local home brews: *chaang* is a refreshing milky ciderlike beverage that can be made from rice, barley, maize or millet; *rakshi* is a hard liquor made from wheat or rice that packs a punch, but is often delicately flavoured with special essences.

Eating Out in Kathmandu

Nepal cannot be considered by any means the gastronomic centre of Asia nevertheless, eating out in Kathmandu is inexpensive and can be pleasurable. Listed below you will find some of the more interesting restaurants. They have been graded as: expensive (over US$15 per head); moderately priced (under US$5–12 per head); or inexpensive (under US$5 per head).

The local beers—*Star, San Miguel* and *Tuborg*—are all good, and the local spirits, especially the rum and vodka, are good mixers and inexpensive compared to the foreign labels.

Kathmandu Restaurants

Expensive

The Ghar-E-Kebab Location: Durbar Marg

One of the most popular restaurants in town, serving some of the best Indian food this side of Delhi. Excellent tandoori and roti cooked in a glass-windowed kitchen. Comfortable surroundings with good Indian classical music to match the ambience. More expensive than most restaurants in Nepal. Includes a bar.

The Chimney Restaurant Location: Hotel Yak and Yeti, Durbar Marg

This was the best known of the restaurants originally run by the legendary Boris. As a tribute to him they still have several items from his original menu, such as borscht, stroganoff or Yeti's Delight. An excellent place for a candle-lit dinner *à deux* with cocktails before and coffee after around circular fireplace. Has a bar.

Hotel Soaltee Holiday Inn Crowne Plaza Location: Kalimati

This five-star hotel provides good-quality restaurants serving western and eastern cuisine. A safe but unadventurous choice. Al Fresco Italian restaurant, by the pool, has probably the best Italian food in town.

Bhaktapur Night Location: Shangrila Hotel, Lazimpath, Kathmandu
A weekly Friday event, weather permitting, when the famous Bhaktapur dances are acted out in a garden that lives up to its name. A candle-lit dinner of exotic oriental

Moderately Priced

Bhancha Ghar Location: Kamaladi
Offers good Nepali cuisine. Situated in an attractively converted old farmhouse consisting of several small rooms and an upstairs bar under the eaves.

KC's Consequence Location: Balaju (follow the signs)
An upmarket version of KC's in Thamel; delicious food in a peaceful outdoor setting around a renovated Nepali farmhouse.

The Old Vienna Inn Location: Entrance to Thamel
A restaurant providing a haven for the homesick Bavarian! Excellent hearty fare, with some of the best schnitzel and strudel in Kathmandu. Daily specials.

Pop Kathmandu Location: Kamaladi (across behind Sherpa Hotel))
One of the few restaurants to serve a good selection of traditional Nepali and Tibetan cuisine. A family concern, brimming with Nepali hospitality.

The Kushi Fuji Location: Durbar Marg
The oldest but still one of the most popular Japanese restaurants, serving typical dishes from an open counter. The lunch sets are excellent value.

The Mountain City Chinese Location: Malla Hotel, Lainchaur
For those who like Chinese food, this restaurant offers good Sichuan specialities and better-than-average Chinese fare. Situated across the courtyard from the hotel.

Summit Hotel—Friday Barbecue Location: Kupendol, Patan
A delightful location overlooking Kathmandu with a panoramic mountain vista. A friendly Nepali-style hotel provides this enjoyable barbecue date with all the trimmings, a friendly atmosphere and moderate prices.

Inexpensive

The Everest Steakhouse Location: Thamel (on the way to Chetrapathi)
A trekkers' paradise! Excellent imported (from as far away as Australia) steak fashioned into an extensive menu from around the world. Great value. The only challenge is to find a seat!

Le Bistro Location: Thamel
An old standby serving typical vegetarian and non-vegetarian fare; big servings and excellent desserts (their chocolate cake is renowned).

The Marco Polo Restaurant Location: Entrance to Thamel
The Italians have made their mark on Thamel too! The best Italian food in town. Wonderful pizzas and bread baked in a clay oven; home-made pastas with delicious sauces.

The Utse Location: Thamel
The oldest surviving restaurant in Kathmandu, serving Tibetan food. *Momos*, meat dumplings fried or steamed, are their speciality.

KC's Location: Thamel
A restaurant famous for its reasonably priced wholesome and varied menus. A favourite amongst world travellers. A worthwhile experience just to meet the legendary KC and to drink the local draft beer, when it is available.

The Nanglo Location: Durbar Marg
One of the most popular venues amongst locals, both Nepali and expatriate. Famous for its sizzler platters on a cold evening around an open fire. The lunchtime local Nepali food is worth a try or, for those who prefer, fish 'n chips are available too. Both indoor and outdoor space and has a bar.

Fuji Restaurant Location: Kantipath, opposite British Council
Located in the grounds of the renowned Royal Hotel in a former concubine's moated residence, where the author Han Suyin once lived. This delightful and picturesque restaurant is certainly worth a visit. They serve great lunch sets and *teriyaki* on the terrace overlooking the moat.

Mike's Breakfast Location: opposite Police Headquarters in Naxal
Mike has moved location (with much of the character and accoutrements from the old concubine's house) to a new and larger destination of similar charm. You can still eat those great breakfasts/brunches al fresco. A great eating and meeting place to get away from it all. Part of the old house has been converted to the **Indigo Gallery**, where you can get an excellent introduction to the art of Nepal. The gallery holds regular art exhibitions and talks by local specialists on Nepal as well as selling unusual art and artifacts from the region.

Him Thai Location: Lazimpat
Recently relocated from Thamel. Authentically fiery Thai food at remarkably low prices.

The Pie Shops of Kathmandu Location: omnipresent in both Thamel Street and Freak Street
Kathmandu has developed a reputation for its pie shops which are to be found on every street corner. Every sort and variety of pastry, flan and tart is available. Months of deprivation add something special to these delicacies—and they certainly make the real thing a great treat on your return home!

Pumpernickel German Bakery Location: Thamel
This bakery serves fresh brown bread, bagels, croissants and is especially popular for its breakfasts of muesli, fruit salad, yoghurt and hot croissants. Also serves a variety of good sandwiches. Pleasant large garden.

Useful Addresses

Police

(Tel. 226998, 211999)

Department of Immigration

Tri Devi Marg; open 10 am to 4 pm; closed Saturdays

General Post Office & Foreign Post Office

Sundhara; open 10 am to 5 pm; closed Saturdays; poste restante to 4 pm only. (Tel 412337)

Airline Offices

Durbar Marg: **Air Canada** (Tel. 222838); **Air France** (Tel. 223339); **Alitalia** (Tel. 220215); **Bangladesh Biman** (Tel. 222544); **Druk Air** (Tel. 225166, 227229); **Indian Airlines** (Tel. 223053); **Japan Airlines** (Tel. 224854); **KLM Royal Dutch Airlines** (Tel. 222895); **Lufthansa** (Tel. 224341); **Pakistan International** (Tel. 2231020; **Singapore Airlines** (Tel. 220759); **Swissair** (Tel. 222452); **Thai International** (Tel. 223565).

Kantipath: **Cathay Pacific** (Tel. 226704); **Air India** (Tel. 212335); **Air Lanka** (Tel. 212831); **Everest Air** (Tel. 229412, 224290); **Korean Air** (Tel. 212080); **Nepal Airways** (Tel. 416575, 418494): **Northwest Airlines** (Tel. 225552); **Qantas** (Tel. 220245); **Royal Nepal Airlines** (Tel. 220757); **Saudi Airlines** (Tel. 222787); **Trans World Airlines** (Tel. 214704).

Embassies and Consulates

Australia, Bansbari (Tel. 411578); **Bangladesh**, Naxal Bhagwati Bahal (Tel. 414943); **China**, Baluwatar (Tel. 411740); **Denmark**, Kantipath (Tel; 227044); **Egypt**, Pulchok, Patan (Tel. 524812); **France**, Lazimpath (Tel. 412332); **Germany**, Gyaneswor (Tel. 221763); **India**, Lainchaur (Tel. 410900); **Israel**, Lazimpath (Tel. 411811); **Italy**, Baluwatar (Tel. 412743); **Japan**, Pani Pokhari (Tel. 414083); **Korea** (North), Patan (Tel. 521084); **Korea** (South), Tahachal (Tel. 270172); **Myanmar** (Burma), Chakupat, Patan Dhoka (Tel. 524788); **Netherlands**, Kumaripati (Tel. 522915); **Pakistan**, Pani Pokhari (Tel.410565); **Sri Lanka**, Kamal Pokhari (Tel. 414192); **Sweden**, Khicha Pokhari (Tel.220939); **Switzerland**, Jawalakhel (Tel. 523468); **Thailand**, Thapathali (Tel. 213910); **United Kingdom**, Lainchaur (Tel. 410590); **USA**, Pani Pokhari (Tel. 411179).

Cultural Centres

British Council, Kantipath (Tel. 221305); **French Cultural Centre**, Bagh Bazaar (Tel. 224326); **Indian Cultural Centre and Library**, RNAC Building, New Road, (Tel. 220757); **Goethe Institute**, Sundhara (Tel. 220528); **US Information Service**, Gyaneshwar (Tel. 415845, 223893).

Tourist Information Centres
Main Office: **Gangapath**, Basantapur (near Hanuman Dhoka), open 10 am to 4 pm, closed Saturday. **Tribhuvan International Airport Exchange** (Tel. 414933); **Department of Tourism** (Tel. 214519, 211293).

Travel Agencies
Adventure Travel Nepal, Durbar Marg (Tel. 221729, 223328); **Annapurna Travel & Tours**, Durbar Marg (Tel. 223940); **Everest Travel Service**, Basantapur (Tel. 222217); **Gorkha Travels**, Durbar Marg (Tel. 224896); **Himalayan Travel & Tours**, Durbar Marg (Tel. 223803); **Kathmandu Travel & Tours**, Tripureswar (Tel. 224536); **Malla Travels**, Malla Hotel (Tel. 410635); **Marco Polo**, Kamal (Tel. 414192); **Natraj Tours & Travels**, Durbar Marg (Tel. 222014); **Nepal Travel Agency**, Ramshahpath (Tel. 412899); **President Travels & Tours**, Durbar Marg (Tel. 220245); **Shanker Travel & Tours**, Lazimpath (Tel. 422565); **Tiger Tops**, Durbar Marg (Tel. 222958, 220507); **Trans Himalayan Tours**, Durbar Marg (Tel. 224854); **Universal Travel & Tours**, Kantipath (Tel. 216080); **World Travels**, Durbar Marg (Tel. 226939); **Yeti Travels**, Durbar Marg (Tel. 221234).

Trekking Agencies
Above the Clouds Trekking, Thamel (Tel. 412921); **Amadablam Trekking**, Lazimpath (Tel. 410219); **Annapurna Mountaineering and Trekking**, Durbar Marg (Tel. 222999); **Asian Trekking**, Kesar Mahal (Tel. 412821); **Great Himalayan Adventures**, Kantipath (Tel. 214424); **Himalayan Adventures**, Lazimpath (Tel. 411477); **Himalayan Journeys**, Kantipath (Tel. 226138); **Himalayan River Exploration**, P.O. Box 170, Naxal (Tel. 418491); **International Trekkers**, Durbar Marg (Tel. 220594); **Lama Excursions**, Durbar Marg (Tel. 220940); **Malla Treks**, Malla Hotel (Tel. 418389); **Manaslu Trekking**, Durbar Marg (Tel. 222422); **Mountain Adventure Trekking**, Thamel (Tel. 414910); **Mountain Travel Nepal**, P.O. Box 170, Naxal (Tel. 414508, 411562); **Natraj Trekking**, Kantipath (Tel. 226644); **Nepal Trekking**, Thamel (Tel. 214681); **Nepal Trekking and Natural History Expeditions**, New Road (Tel. 222489); **Rover Treks & Expeditions**, Naxal (Tel. 414373); **Sherpa Cooperative Trekking**, Durbar Marg (Tel. 224068); **Sherpa Trekking Service**, Kamaladi (Tel. 222489); **Trans-Himalayan Trekking**, Durbar Marg (Tel. 223854).

Foreign Organizations
U.N. Agencies, U.N. Building, Pulchok, Patan (Tel. 523200-11); **UNDP**, Pulchok, Patan (Tel. 523220-11); **British Transit Camp**, Jawalakhel, Lalitpur (Tel. 521211); **British Volunteer Service**, Lazimpath (Tel. 415644); **Care Nepal**, Pulchok, Lalitpur PO Box 1661 (Tel. 522143); **Danish Volunteer Service**, Dillibazar, Kathmandu PO Box 4010 (Tel. 410040); **FAO**, UN Building, Pulchok, Patan (Tel. 523200-11); **German Development Service**, Bhat Bhateni (Tel. 414352); **GTZ**,

Pulchok, Patan (Tel. 523228); **ICIMOD**, Jawalakhel, Lalitpur PO Box 3226 (Tel. 522839); **JOVC** (Japan Overseas Volunteers Corporation), Patan, Lalitpur PO Box 264 (Tel. 522211); **SATA**, Jawalakhel, Lalitpur PO Box 113 (Tel. 521205); **Save the Children Federation**, Maharajgunj, Kathmandu (Tel. 412447); **SNV** (Netherlands Development Organization), Jawalakhel, Lalitpur PO Box 1966 (Tel. 522915); **UNICEF**, Pulchok, Patan (Tel. 522857); **United Mission of Nepal**, Thapathali (Tel. 212179); **US Aid**, Kalimati (Tel. 270144); **US Peace Corps**, Kalimadi (Tel. 410019); **WHO**, UN Building, Pulchok, Patan (Tel. 523200-11).

Rescue

Himalayan Rescue Association (Tel. 418755) in the grounds of the Kathmandu Guest House. Open 11 am to 5 pm Sunday to Friday. Staffed by volunteers from overseas and with a small library of reference books, this is a mine of information about trekking conditions, health precautions and medical aid.

Practical information, such as telephone numbers, opening hours and hotel and restaurant prices, is notoriously subject to being outdated by changes or inflation. We welcome corrections and suggestions from guidebook users; please write to The Guidebook Company, 20 Hollywood Road, Hong Kong.

Appendices

Historical Figures

Abjayaraja Sakya	builder of Mahabaudha in Patan
Amsuvarnam	Hindu king
Ashoka	Mauryan emperor of Northern India
Bhimsen Thapa	prime minister 1806–37
Birendra Bir Bikram Shah Dev	Mahendra's son and present ruler; born 28 December 1945
Chakrabartindra	son of Pratap Malla
Chandra Shumsher Rana	prime minister 1914–68
Charumati	daughter of Ashoka
Halarchan Dev	built the Min Nath in Patan, 16th century
Jaimal	a famous wrestler of Bhaktapur
Kangma	girl of supernatural birth, mythical builder of Baudhanath *stupa* at Sankhu
Kishor Narsingh and Kumar Narsingh	skilled engineers employed by Chandra Shumsher Rana to construct the Singha Durbar
Mahapatra Jagatpal Varma	founded Jagat Pal Vihara near Kirtipur in 1514
Narendradev, King	founder of Bungamati in 1593
Patta	one of the famous wrestlers of Bhaktapur
Purandharsingha	built Char Narayan Mandir in 1566, Hanuman devoted to him
Shankardeva	legendary king who established Sankhu
Tripura Sundari	wife of Rana Bahadur Shah
Yogamati	daughter of Yogendra Malla

Kings of Nepal

Early Malla Rulers of the Valley

Ari Malla (or Arideva)	1200–36
Abhaya Malla	1236–55
Jayadeva, ruled Patan and Kathmandu	1255–8
Anandadeva, ruled Bhadgaon	1255–?
Jayabhimadeva	1258–71
Jayasimha Malla	1271–4
Ananta Malla	1274–1310
Jayanadadeva	1310–28
Jayari Malla	1320–44
Jayarajdeva	1347–54 (d.1360)
Jayastithi Malla	1354–95
Dharma Malla, Jyotir Malla, Kirti Malla	1395–1428 (joint rule)
Yaksha Malla	1428–82

Rulers of Bhaktapur

Raya Malla (son of Yaksha Malla)	1481–1512
Bhuban Malla	1512–?
Prana Malla, Jit Malla	?–1547
Viswa Malla	1547–?
Trailokya Malla	?–1613
Jagat Jyoti Malla	1613–37
Naresh Malla	1637–44
Jagatprakash Malla	1644–72
Jitamitra Malla	1673–96
Bhupatindra Malla	1696–1722
Ranajit Malla	1722–69

(surrendered to Prithvi Narayan Shah)

Rulers of Lalitpur

Visnu Simha	?–1565
Nara Simha, Uddhav Simha, Purandar Simha	1565–9 (joint rule)
Purandar Simha	1569–97
Harihar Simha Malla (son of Kathmandu king)	1597–1618
Siddhi Narasimha Malla	1618–60 (d.1661)
Srinivas Malla	1660–84

Yoganarendra Malla	1684–1705
Lokaprakash Malla	?
Indra Malla	?
Birnar Simha	?
Mahendra Malla	?
Riddinar Sing	?
Mahendra Simha (Bhasker Malla of Kantipur	?–1722
Yogaprakash Malla	1722–86

Rulers of Kathmandu (Kantipur)

Ratan Malla (son of Yaksha Malla)	1484–1520
Surya Malla	1520–9
Amar Malla (also known as Narendra Malla)	1529–60
Mahendra Malla	1560–79
Sadasiva Malla	1580–9 (banished)
Siva Simha Malla	1589–1618
Laxmi Narsimha Malla	1618–41
Pratap Malla	1641–74
Nipendra Malla	1674–80
Parthibendra Malla	1680–7
Bhupalendra Malla	1687–1700
Basker Malla	1700–22
Jagaj Jaya Malla	1722–34
Jayaprakash Malla	1734–68 (defeated by Prithvi Narayan Shah)

The Shah Rulers of Gorkha

Drabya Shah	1559–70
Purandar Shah	1570–1605
Chhetra Shah	1606
Rama Shah	1606–33
Dambar Shah	1633–44
Krishna Shah	?
Rudra Shah	?
Prithvipati Shah	1669–1716
Narabhupal Shah	1716–42
Prithvi Narayan Shah	1742–74

Glossary

agam	private house god
avatar	an incarnation
bahal	style of Buddhist monastery
bahil	style of Buddhist monastery
bhajan	religious musical gathering
chaitya	small *stupa*
chaku	part of *stupa*, square base to the pinnacle
chapara	pilgrim's resthouse
chowk	square courtyard
dharmashala	public resthouse
dyochhen	god house
gajur	pinnacle on the top roof of a temple
guthi	a religious body responsible for upkeep of festival rituals and temples
hiti	tank
homa	type of Buddhist worship performed by a Bajacharya priest
jhingati	type of roof tile
kailash	copper pot
karma	the belief that consequences of past actions are realized in future lives
kumari	a young girl, yet to reach puberty, selected as a goddess by the Sakye cast. Participant in major Hindu festivals. There are *kumaris* in all main towns in the Valley.
lingam	Hindu phallic symbol, associated with Shiva
mahanta	chief priest
mandapa	town assembly hall
mantra	written Buddhist prayers
math	Nepali–Hindu priest house
mela	great fair
namaste	traditional greeting or blessing made by placing hands together in front of face and bowing. Equivalent of shaking hands in West
namarkar	same as *namaste*, but more exaggerated and showing reverence to senior members of the community
nag	sacred serpent
nirvana	Buddhist belief that desire comes to an end in *nirvana*; achieved by the eightfold path
panch ratna	five precious stones usually associated with the religious foundations of buildings

pathi	resthouse
puja	Hindu worship, welcoming a god to the company of its worshippers
purna kalasha	sacred pot in Annapurna temple
rath	towering temple chariot
sadhu	holy man
saldup	resinous mixture used to seal joints in brickwork
sattal	resthouse, as well as long-term dwelling place for members of religious communities
shankha	conch shell
shikhara	a tower-like temple style imported from India
stupa	a hemispherical solid mound usually enshrining a relic of the Buddha; has gilded pinnacle over it
telia	wedge-shaped brick used during the Malla era; method recreated for author's restoration projects
tikka	an outward sign, usually red, on the forehead to denote a visit made to a temple for washing
tol	district within a town
torana	carved pediment over entrance to a religious building or palace
trisul	metal trident, symbol of Shiva
tunasi	roof struts
vajra	sacred thunderbolt
vihara	Buddhist monastery or temple
yoni	'source', symbol of the female organ, found in combination with *lingam*

Divinities

Agamdevta	secret house goddess
Annapurna	goddess; provider of food; a beneficent form of Durga
Arjuna	archer; one of five Pandava princes in the *Mahabharata*
Astabhairabs	eight bhairabs
Astamatrikas	eight matrikas
Astanagas	eight nagas
Avaloketesvara	the tutelary deity of Nepal
Bhadrakali	Hindu goddess; a form of Durga
Bhagawati Mahishamardini	a lesser Hindu divinity
Bhairab	one of the personifications of Shiva's energy
Bhimsen	Hindu protector and promoter of trades and crafts
Bishwakarma	Hindu god of craftsmen
Brahma	god of creation
Buddha	the enlightened or awakened one
Bundyo of Bungamati	Machhendranath
Byhagrini	tigress daughter
Chandeswari	the local name for Parvati as the slayer of Chand, a fearful demon
Dashavatar of Vishnu	the ten incarnations of Vishnu
Devi	all-embracing female divinity; a general term for a goddess
Dharmaraj	King of Justice, the embodiment of Dharma
Draupadi	a daughter of Drupada, King of Pancala, in the *Mahabharata*; wife of the five Pandava brothers
Durga	composite goddess; fearful aspect of Shiva
Five Dhyani Buddhas	appear in meditation in Vajrayana Buddhism
Ganesh	benevolent elephant-headed god of wisdom. Son of Shiva and Parvati. A problem-solver and revered by all Hindus.
Ganga	name of the Ganges and its personification as a goddess
Goraknath	a *yogin* of the Natha cult
Gujeswari	Shiva's spouse
Gunkamadeva	controlled the *nags* to appease gods after committing misdemeanours
Hanuman	monkey god, ally of Rama in war against Ravana

Hari Shankar	a combined form of Vishnu and Shiva
Harihar Bahan Lokeswar	Buddhist version of Vishnu
Hiranyaksha	demon
Indra	Hindu god of rain
Janmadye	*see* Padmapani Avaloketeswar
Jaya	one of the two gatekeepers of Vishnu's palace
Kali	fearful goddess, aspect of Shiva, a giver and destroyer of life usually depicted as a hideous four-armed emaciated woman who devours all beings
Krishna	ideal youth, lover and statesman; one of Vishnu's incarnations
Kumari	living goddess; incarnation of Taleju
Lakshmi (Laxmi)	goddess of wealth and prosperity; wife of Narayan
Lakshminarayan	Lakshmi and Narayan (Vishnu) conjoined
Machhendranath	*see* Padmapani Avaloketeswar
Manjusri	a Bodhisattva in the Buddhist pantheon; partner of Saraswati
Mantraja	favourite house goddess of Shrinivasa Malla
Nandi	bull; Shiva's celestial vehicle
Narasimha	man-lion; one of Vishnu's nine incarnations
Narayan	name for Vishnu
Navadurga	the nine forms of Durga
Padmapani Avaloketeswar	the most compassionate divinity (commonly known as Janmadye or Machhendranath)
Parvati	consort of Shiva
Pashupati	lord of animals and protector of the Valley; one of Shiva's most venerated forms
Rama	hero of Ramayana; part incarnation of Vishnu
Ram Chandra	*see* Rama
Ravana of Lanka	demon king; vanquished by Ram Chandra
Rukmini	wife of Krishna and one of his two favourite *gopinis*; an incarnation of Lakshmi
Saraswati	Hindu goddess of learning; partner of Manjusri
Satyabhama	one of Krishna's wives
Shaivas	followers of Shiva
Shantikar	helped Gunkamadeva to control the *nags*
Shiva	god; destroyer and rejuvenator
Siddharta Gautama	name of the prince born at Lumbini in 553 BC before achieving enlightenment and becoming known as the Buddha

Simhini	lion son
Sita	the human form of Lakshmi
Surya	the sun god
Uma	daughter of Himalaya; beneficent aspect of Shiva
Vaintej	human-faced Garuda
Vaishnavas	followers of Vishnu
Varaha	boar; one of Vishnu's nine incarnations
Vipssaya Buddha	Buddha; fabled to have thrown lotus in Kathmandu Valley Lake to reveal Swayambhu
Vishnu	Hindu god; preserver of life
Visvabhu Buddha	prophesied the prosperity of the Valley
Visvakarma	form of Manjusri
Vyangini	minor Hindu deity
Yama	ruler and judge of the dead

Recommended Reading

General

Bista, D.B. *People of Nepal* (Kathmandu: Ratna Pustak Bhandar, 1987).

Fleming, R.L. Sr., Fleming, R.L. Jr. and Bangdel, L. *Birds of Nepal* (Kathmandu: Avalok, 1979).

Hari, A.M. *Conversational Nepali* (Kathmandu: Summer Institute of Linguistics, 1971).

Lall, K. *Lore and Legend of Nepal* (Kathmandu: Ratna Pustak Bhandar, 1976).

Lall, K. *Nepalese Customs and Manners* (Kathmandu: Ratna Pustak Bhandar, 1976).

Mierow, D. and Shrestha, T.B. *Himalayan Flowers and Trees* (Kathmandu: Sahayogi Prakashan, 1978).

Moran, K. *Nepal Handbook* (Chico: Moon Publications 1991).

Shrestha, S.H. *Simple Georgraphy of Nepal* (Kathmandu: Educational Enterprise, 1983).

Vaidya, K. *Folk Tales of Nepal* (Kathmandu: Ratna Pustak Bhandar, 1980).

History

Fisher, M.W. *The Political History of Nepal* (Berkeley: University of California, Institute of International Studies, 1960).

Rana, Pudma Jung Bahadur. *Life of Maharaja Sir Jung Bahadur of Nepal* (Allahabad, India: Pioneer Press, 1909).

Snellgrove, D. and Richardson, H. *A Cultural History of Tibet* (Boulder, Colorado: Prajna Press, 1980).

Stiller, L.F. *The Rise of the House of Gorkha* (New Delhi: Manjusri, 1973).

Stiller, L.F. *The Silent Cry* (Kathmandu: Sahayogi Prakashan, 1976).

Religion and Festivals

Anderson, M.M. *Festivals of Nepal* (London: George Allen and Unwin, 1971).

Blofeld, J. *The Tantric Mysticism of Tibet* (Boulder, Colorado: Prajna Press, 1982).

Conze, E. *Buddhism, Its Essence and Development* (Oxford: Bruno Cassirer, 1951).

Deep, D.K. *The Nepal Festivals* (Kathmandu: Ratna Pustak Bhandar, 1982).

Detmold, G. and Rubel, M. *The Gods and Goddesses of Nepal* (Kathmandu: Ratna Pustak Bhandar, 1979).

Sen, K.M. *Hinduism* (Harmondsworth: Penguin Books, 1961).

Snellgrove, D. *Buddhist Himalaya* (Oxford: Bruno Cassirer, 1957).

Art and Architecture

Aran, L. *The Art of Nepal* (Kathmandu: Sahayogi Prakashan, 1978).
Haaland, A. *Bhaktapur: a changing town* (Kathmandu; 1982)
Korn, W. *The Traditional Architecture of the Kathmandu Valley* (Kathmandu: Ratna Pustak Bhandar, 1977).
Kramrisch, S. *The Art of Nepal* (New York, 1964).
Macdonald, W.W. and Vergati Stahl, A. *Newar Art* (New Delhi: Vikas, 1979).
Nepali, G.S. *The Newars, An Ethno-Sociological Study of a Himalayan Community* (Bombay: United Asia Publications, 1965).
Pruscha, C. *Kathmandu Valley: The Preservation of Physical Environment and Cultural Heritage, A Protective Inventory* (Vienna: Anton Schroll, 1975). Two volumes.
Sanday, J. *The Hanuman Dhoka Royal Palace, Kathmandu: Building Conservation and Local Traditional Crafts* (London: AARP, 1974).
Singh, M. *Himalayan Arts* (London: UNESCO, 1968).

Photography

Amin, M., Willets, D. and Tetley, B. *Journey Through Nepal* (London: Bodley Head, 1987).
Sansoni, D. and Goodman, J. *Kathmandu* (Singapore: Times Editions, 1978).
Wassman, B. and Van Beek, S. *Our World in Colour: Nepal* (Hong Kong: The Guidebook Company Ltd, 1989).

Index

ISGB/12/03